S0-AGT-706

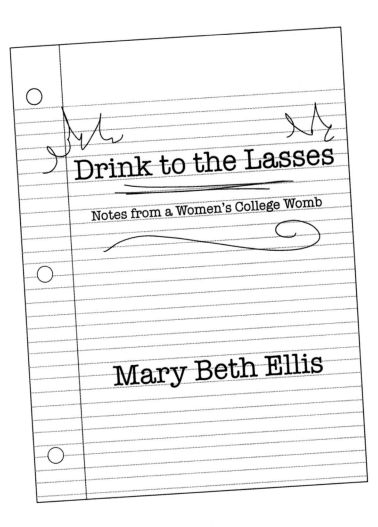

Drink to the Lasses

Notes from a Women's College Womb

Mary Beth Ellis

Cold Tree Press
Nashville, Tennessee

Published by Cold Tree Press
Nashville, Tennessee
www.coldtreepress.com

© 2006 Mary Beth Ellis. All rights reserved.
Cover photographs property of Mary Beth Ellis.
Cover and Page Design by Amanda Butler © 2006 Cold Tree Press
This book may not be reproduced in any form without express written permission.

Printed in the United States of America
ISBN 1-58385-106-2

*For Mom and Dad,
who loaded the van, drove it
five hours north, and loved me
enough to hug me goodbye and
get right back in and leave me
to the Belles and the Domers
and the cracks in the sidewalk.*

*And much love and gratitude
to Our Lady, because even if
a brother and sister have a
nuclear-grade fight over who
gets the seat by the window,
they will always have their
Mother in common.*

Here's to the Freshman, verdant and green
Here's to the Sophomore, naughty
Here's to the Junior, fair, youthful queen,
Here's to the Senior, haughty
Toast with your glasses
Drink to the lasses
We'll warrant each proves a delight to her classes.

Popular women's academy toast, circa 1900

This is a true story...

With a whole bunch of paragraph breaks added in.

What you are about to experience, may God have mercy on your soul, is not intended as a scholarly exploration of Catholic women's colleges, or a complete and accurate portrayal of these remarkable ladies known as Saint Mary's students, or a treatise on campus life in Ye Olde Mid-To-Late 1990's; so knives down. If I learned anything about Saint Mary's at Saint Mary's, it is that we cannot get enough of discussing ourselves, and whether we like ourselves, and whether *others* like ourselves, and what our butt looks like in these pants, and what the Pope says about it, and what Betty Friedan says about it, and how, in the end, we shouldn't *care* about what our butt looks like in these pants, for this is a Western patriarchal expectation of female attractiveness designed to *keep The Woman down.* Tea?

The school is neither a lesbian commune nor a convent, which is how most people, depending upon their gender, tend to react when I announce that I did my undergraduate work at a women's college. The full-turn panoramic truth lies somewhere in the middle, a sort of convent commune, if you will; most of us compared Noxema–soaked notes on men as eighteen-year-olds tend to do, but usually in between working on essays discussing the virgin-whore dichotomy in Steinbeck novels.

There exists a Notre Dame-born stereotype that all a Saint Mary's student is good for is hoisting into the air her cleavage, two piña coladas, and her legs, but this demands coordination I have yet to attain. Some Saint Mary's women, when the question of *"Why... in the world... would you..."* arises from the general public, rise to the defensive: "It's just like any other college," they'll say, when... it's not. It takes a certain woman to attend a women's college. You have to be prepared, for instance, for the academic reality of twenty female voices in a freshman German class repeating: *"Eine Currywurst, bitte.* A curried sausage, please."

In any case, the vast majority of Saint Mary's women, unlike the author, do not arrive on campus completely male-fearing, with a raging case of as-yet undiagnosed obsessive compulsive disorder and a complete inability to add in their heads. Some actually use such sentences as "I would like to dialogue with you on this"; some prefer "Get out of the way, you're blocking my automatic weapon." Most are simply walking to chemistry class.

I just know what happened to me, and what happened to me was a phone call from the Notre Dame Leprechaun and a great deal of slicing apart a fetal pig, only not necessarily at the same time, although this would make for an outstanding *Lifetime* Movie Of the Week. Signing my early-admissions contract with Saint Mary's still stands as the best decision I have ever made—and my life is rich with good decisions, such as the time I refused a date with a person wearing a sunvisor sideways and a tee shirt that read "ASK ME ABOUT MY BEER NUTS."

You may notice that I do not include a description of Notre Dame football games in these pages. This is not because I don't care or harbor animosity towards my brother school. Rather, I wish to highlight the fact that life at Saint Mary's and Notre Dame is about so much more than football. It is also about standing around in very hot rooms with very loud music, yelling "WHAT?"

Besides, the football picture was constantly shifting. Notre Dame Stadium was renovated during my era, with the addition of twenty thousand extra seats and a whole world of concrete. Lou Holtz was the head football coach until I was a sophomore, and then he left and the campus newspaper printed a full-page color picture of him with an enormous black background that read "LOU HOLTZ, 1986-1996," like he died or something. He very well may have, given the two seasons that followed.

And anyway the best description I ever saw of a home football game consisted of a picture I once took of a morning-after campus trash can overflowing with beer detritus and glowingly empty liquor bottles.

I refer to this period as the best four years of my life, and it was, but not in the way most people assume. I did not pass eight semesters in an alcoholic stupor (I couldn't afford it) or locked in the library, weeping as I performed literary exegesis on the lesser works of Sylvia Plath (I couldn't stand it.) Between the ages of eighteen and twenty-two I slammed doors and kissed exactly the wrong people at precisely the wrong time and settled upon myself as the focal point of each building I stood within and every tree I walked beneath. I did things that I in my high school uniform jumper did not think myself was capable of; stripped my soul down to its orderly Catholic neutrons and blew the whole smash apart. I knelt down in the Indiana gravel, appalled, and scraped it back together as best I could. And then I went to my Latin American Policy discussion lab.

I came away with a piece of paper certifying my BA and a page in my journal that said man, there is a world out here and you had better know how to write a thank-you note in it.

None of this is in the yearbook.

✳ ✳ ✳

Baby versions of portions of this book appeared as columns in *The Observer*, the Notre Dame-Saint Mary's student newspaper, because I am in fact just that lazy. Also aged. I don't know that I'd fully recall specific events without consulting old, bad writing.

I remembered as accurately and as lovingly as I could. There are real people in this book (whose names I changed), real events (which I put rouge on to make less bourgeois than they actually were—for that is truly what I am, you see, a great big ol' ball of bourgeois), and real buildings (many of which are now failed Trump casinos). Bottom line: I'm pretty sure Saint Mary's College and the University of Notre Dame actually exist. I'll check on it and get back to you.

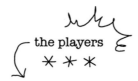

the players
✳ ✳ ✳

Saint Mary's College: My college. It is a women's college. It has a lake. You would like it.

The University of Notre Dame: Saint Mary's across-the-street brother school. Perhaps you've heard of it. It has *two* lakes.

Belles: Sports nickname of Saint Mary's College. Okay, if you and I are going to get along, as author and reader, you are going to have to trust me. And your first act of trust is to believe me when I tell you that a grown-up group of people—academics— decided that a really super-great, pride-inspiring nickname for a volleyball team would be... the Belles.

The Avenue: Road connecting Saint Mary's to Notre Dame. Excellent for in-line skating. Bad for the grade point average.

SMC: Pronounced "smick." References a student of Saint Mary's. We can say it, but you can't.

Anne: Corridormate, freshman year. Roommate, sophomore year. Mortal enemy, second day of sophomore year.

SYR: A "Screw Your Roommate" dance was predicated on drafting blind dates via friends and roommates. This often resulted in an alcohol-soaked arranged marriage with a duration of perhaps four hours, which culminated in drunken, grabby not-sex and never speaking to the lady or gentleman in question again.

Carah: Best friend and dormmate, freshman year. Said things like, "A blinking light on your answering machine means somebody loves you!" and you didn't even want to hit her.

Hemingway: Stuffed pelican. When you go away to a big adult college with a big adult dorm room, a stuffed pelican is necessary for protection.

Frances Davidson Trenton: First dance date. See: University of Notre Dame Glee Club

Detex: May be used as a noun or a verb. Refers to working within the security system of the Saint Mary's dorms, often unsuccessfully.

Kathy: Corridormate, freshman year. Slept perhaps a grand total of twenty minutes in four years.

Parietals: Rule on both campii stipulating that the opposite sex was to have vacated the dorms at midnight on weeknights and two AM on weekends. Because, as we all know, sex only happens before PBS goes off the air for the night.

Amy: Next door neighbor, freshman year. Posted a sign on her door covered with a grand round-up of every euphemism I'd ever heard, and some I wished I'd never heard, for "drunk." This is pretty much all you need to know about Amy.

Holy Cross Hall: My sophomore home. It was old and not very fireproof, but the banisters in the main foyer (it had a *foyer*) were eminently slidable, and you could launch a large-to-medium-sized cannon from the long narrow windows. I will not elaborate further.

Patty: Corridormate, freshman year. *She* had an anatomically correct poster of Mickey Mouse on the front of her door.

The Observer: Shared student paper between Saint Mary's and Notre Dame. I wrote for it all the way through my college career, plus an extra year past graduation. Then it got better.

Edmonds: Corridormate, freshman year. Able to be heard in distant galaxies.

The Grotto: Shrine to Our Lady of Lourdes at Notre Dame. It is very rock-intensive, and very pretty. You're supposed to shove money in a metal box and light a candle. I never had quarters, so I would always prayer-steal off somebody else's. Mary didn't seem to mind all that much.

Two North: As in the second floor, North tower, of Regina Hall. Collective reference to corridormates-at-arms.

Dead Fetal Pig: Dead Fetal Pig, I barely knew ye. I dissected thee for my freshman bio class so that I would gain a deep understanding and appreciation for the delicate miracles God works in each and every morsel of nature. Alas, you died in vain.

Justine: Corridormate, freshman year. As a sophomore, her advanced age—nineteen—established her as the corridor matriarch. From Cleveland, a fact she managed to overcome.

Basilica of the Sacred Heart: Ridiculously beautiful church on Notre Dame's campus. Between the statues and the stained glass and the eight skillion liturgical doodads, it looks like the Vatican is holding a yard sale on the perfectly-gilded inside, and if you would like to get married in there, good freaking luck.

Grace: Corridormate, Freshman year. Four feet tall and in the Army.

Regina Hall: Freshman dorm. Room 212. Regina used to be a convent. Regina shows it. A single room in Regina afforded precisely enough space for a loft bed, a crucifix, and your guilt.

University of Notre Dame Glee Club: All-male, fifty-member a cappella chorus. You made a woman out of me, Glee Club. I wish I knew how to quit you.

LeMans Hall: Saint Mary's major administrative building, home to LeMans Bell Tower, which, in grad school, after much wrenching, I described as "a warm, square beige against the tired South Bend sky." I was very deep back then. Also, insufferable.

The Notre Dame Leprechaun: 1. (verb) Living student mascot for the Fighting Irish. He gets hoisted up in the air during football games, okay, and he does pushups for however many points Notre Dame has. 2. (noun) My first date.

U.S. Route 33: Dividing line between Saint Mary's and Notre Dame property. You can stand in the middle of this road for four years, as I did, although this can get you pulverized, as I was. It is highly recommended.

Indiana, The State Of: Large, flat area between Ohio and Illinois containing endless amounts of cornfields here and livestock there, the monotony of which was regularly broken by livestock standing in cornfields. Contains Saint Mary's and Notre Dame in the northern sector.

Papa John's Pizza Breadstick: Left over from 2 AM study session in Regina Hall in 1995 and duct-taped to the bathroom wall. Quite possibly still there.

LaFortune Student Center: Hub of Domer activity at Notre Dame. The proper pronunciation is "La FOUR-Chun." I would recommend that you do not pronounce it on campus as "La Four-TOON" to people you are attempting to impress. I will not elaborate further.

My Obsessive Compulsive Disorder: Hold on a sec, I have to go wash my hands.

Domer: Slang for a student at the University of Notre Dame. Someone with a bachelor and a Master's from the University is called a "Double Domer," and you should never, ever, approach the subject of student loans. In its most technical sense, "Domer" refers to a male student. Females are traditionally called "Damers," although this might get you shot when used in the wrong place at the wrong time.

Mary Beth Ellis: Here are my measurements:

SAT: 1080

ACT: 32

GPA: 3.6

Number of people who currently care about these things: 0

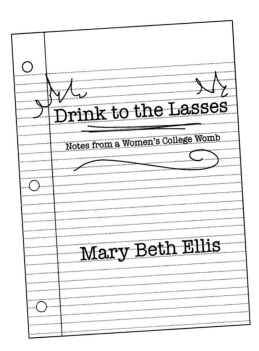

Drink to the Lasses

Notes from a Women's College Womb

Mary Beth Ellis

chapter one
✳ ✳ ✳

Tunnels

Там here were tunnels beneath my school, subterraneous veins
through which only students and the mostly-female staff were
allowed to flow. It was dark down there, and drippy, but ninety
percent of the time this was preferable to the South Bend weather
aboveground.

Our brother school had the Good Year Blimp seven Saturdays
a year, but we had this, the ability to walk below tree roots and
emerge squinting in the weak winter sunlight. The tunnels
connected dorm to bookstore to library, and the roaring stuffiness
was sometimes so intense around the hot water lines that often
when I emerged land-side to take on the last few hundred feet
between me and the classroom building, I stepped into the biting
outside air bareheaded, sweatshirt sleeves pushed up and carrying
my stadium jacket through the falling snow.

Some artistic souls took to decorating the tunnels; murals,
club advertisements, class signatures. So every fifty yards or so
would go like this: Grey grey grey *enormous blue French Cross;* grey
grey grey *quote from former College president;* grey grey grey *Look!
Multicolored wrestling worms! It's Art!* grey grey grey...And there
were spiders anyway.

Some said the tunnels were haunted. The only ancient spirit I
experienced was that of an aged nun's. I was caught behind her

1

at a shaft in the system in which the tunnels were too narrow to pass; I trailed her all the way across campus, underground, weaving behind, room keys clicking impatiently against my backpack. Her ankles were fiberoptic thin, spaghetti strands in support hose. I stared at the backs of her sensible shoes as I tailgated her in my tattered sneakers. Move! Move! *Move!* I was eighteen! With *things* to do!

She reached the end of the corridor, touched the door, turned back to smile at me, then slid past and walked back the other way.

The tunnels were glorious stealth, an echoey form of transport. We liked walking unseen. It could be midnight, one AM, four; we were still able to glide silently through the campus without the night ever knowing about it.

We laid our honor down before the tunnels. Parietals, we snapped with the ease of a Pixy Stick. There was an... understanding about that; we felt it was a stupid rule, and so we massaged our actions around it, when necessary. Man In the Tunnels, there was an understanding about that, too. Dates were rarely taken for a tour.

The administration shut down the tunnels soon after I graduated. Security risk, they said; codes, and regulations, and all. When I read the news, I sat back in my big-girl, real-world chair, sorrowing. The students who have since taken my place wear their jackets all the time now.

I bet that nun's still down there.

chapter two

* * *

HELLO MY NAME IS

The Catholic Church doesn't teach much about Purgatory anymore, preferring instead to stage it live on Earth in the form of Freshman Orientation at its institutions of higher learning. It is boot camp for middle-upper class Catholics, a terrible suspension between life at home and life at college—we were physically *at* college, on the campus, but the administration felt that we couldn't handle the equipment yet, and so held us captive for three days talking us to death about The College Experience while refusing to actually let us have it.

There was a lot of welcoming going on; I was vomitously tired of being greeted, and smiled at, and in general oriented. There was a great deal of emphasis on our choice of a women's school, and yay us, because studies showed that women's school graduates showed higher incidences of going on to advanced degrees and creating their own companies and wrestling rhinoceroses or whatever. As the alumna of an all-female Catholic high school, this was not news to me; what I was curious about was how long it took entire dorms to synchronize to the same menstrual cycle.

"You will gather for Mass here twice in your career at Saint Mary's," we'd been told by an administrator it had been difficult to take seriously, standing as he was in front of an altar backdrop that seemed to be the result of an explosion in a Crayola factory.

"Your Freshman Orientation Mass today welcomes you, and your Baccalaureate Mass four years from now will bid you farewell." Well, four years is a long time to stand in line at the registrar's office, brother. I looked around at the lurching sea of unfamiliar female faces accompanied by phalanxes of family members, all wearing identically murderous "Why couldn't she just have gone to community college?" expressions.

When I checked in at Saint Mary's, I was given: a room key, a mailbox key, a student ID form, a Notre Dame football ticket application, a housing contract, the College handbook, the College mission statement, an Orientation schedule, a class schedule, and a blue-bordered nametag. HELLO MY NAME IS.

The air was dense with antiseptic and bitten fingernails and August humidity thick like caramel. What had been bucolic with a steady academic thrum during my admission interview in the previous October was now a war zone.

"This is the one," I'd announced to my parents as a high school senior while we lunched at Saint Mary's student snack bar. Turkey on croissant, no lettuce. Most of it wound up in shreds on my plate. I had dragged them campus to campus across the entire Tri-State area for the past three years, from Purdue to Bowling Green to a tiny rundown school in Armpit, Ohio, which had a brochure that touted "the new computer" and where my parents told me I would have to go to college if I was bad.

"If this is what you think you need," my mother said. She went to a women's college, too. She looked at my father—who had not—and said, "So?"

He thought for a minute, mulling over his fries. "This is a good cheeseburger," he said finally. "Okay. You can go here." And the sun came out and tiny little animated birds sang from the windowsill, and whatever else happens when your life locks in and you don't even feel nauseated about it.

And, well, *now* the whole joint was under siege by an armada of minivans. There were shower totes in the flower beds, futon parts scattered on the lawns, sobbing refugees wandering the quads. The bookstore looked like the aftermath of the military coup of a small South American nation.

The bubbling relief of finding the right college vanished in the humid, obstacle-course act of actually moving there. That specific instant, I believe, arrived the moment the dorm elevator broke down while the vast majority of the boxes were still in the car.

There were picnics and open houses and endless, humiliating icebreaker games. Also fake emergencies: Late one night some evil fool pulled Regina's fire alarm. So the Worst Noise In the World flooded the corridors, shrieking off the concrete walls, destroying the human soul, and we poured out onto the nearest lawn in dorm shirts and bad hair.

"If this is another one of those blank-damned icebreakers," a girl flopped down on the grass next to me muttered, "I'm *transferring.*"

✳ ✳ ✳

When we were allowed back inside I lay in my loft bed between stiff new sheets, staring at the ceiling, which was two inches away from my face. I struggled to sleep; we had a lecture on Dental Hygiene At the College Level at 8 AM. Then, and only then, could the best four years of our lives commence.

I gazed at dark brown splotches in irregular places. It looked like a cow exploded. What *was* that? How did it come to be, way up here on the ceiling?

And…how did such a tiny room hold such an immense amount of heat? Stupid bloody *bed on stilts*—I raised myself on my elbows to push away my sheets. Tomorrow I was going to have to—

There followed the type of thud you hear before you feel: I had achieved the feat of banging my head on the ceiling by sitting up in bed. Wary of tumbling to the box-strewn floor below, I lay down again, vertebra on vertebra. The sheets were fine where they were.

✳ ✳ ✳

I managed to upgrade the condition of my room to that of Federal Disaster Area Warranting, at Minimum, a Vice Presidential Visit when my parents uncurled me from the fetal position I had assumed amongst the boxes to say goodbye.

I walked them to the van; having never stayed away from home for longer than a week, I didn't know if they could handle the separation. Fifty-four year olds are at a very difficult stage.

They had learned from my older sister's orientation that the best strategy was one of dump-and-run. You show up, unpack, wait for a Planned Activity, and *drive!drive!drive!* This did not issue from a lack of love or concern, but the firm belief that a protracted, keening good-bye with feint departures and Hallmark pronouncements flung from the minivan window simply delayed the rending of the Band-Aid.

We are German. Scenes are for liquor-drinking people.

So they hugged me goodbye and they got in the van and they *left* me there, which is perhaps the best thing, as parents, that they have ever done—leaving me to the registrar and the Monet posters and the straight thin lines of the textbooks. What grips me now as I stand looking over the shoulder of my hairsprayed self was that they *knew,* as I didn't, what was about to happen to me… they knew that I would never again consider the house I grew up in as crux of the universe around which all planets and God Himself rotated.

I think they got their money's worth.

✳ ✳ ✳

You should know that I pretty much hate people. I require time to myself in the same way that other human beings require oxygen. And I had just spent the last three days with *hoards* of *people,* people I do not know, people who as a matter of self-defense sorted me as "Regina, Cincinnati, English Writing." I had to inhale or

6

register for firearms.

So on the last night of Orientation I stood in my Regina cell, inhaling. I had a wad of adhesive in one hand and a color picture of John Adams in the other. Jimmy Buffett announced that he was looking at forty from the stereo on the dust-covered floor. An open can of Cherry Coke sat on my desk amidst a sea of thank-you notes, envelopes included, and erasable pens still in the package.

I was also Not Participating.

Earlier in the day I'd overheard two of my corridormates in a conversation about an Orientation safety seminar—"How Not To Get Lured Into the Back of a Van and Chopped Into Little Tiny Pieces" or some such, to be immediately followed by a forum session entitled "Multiculturalism Awareness Training: Meet The Two Black Students"—and one said, "You going?" and the other said, "Nah, let's watch a movie instead."

I lifted my head, mid-fetal position: What was this? They... weren't following the schedule? But... we had an Orientation Schedule! It was on paper! With a cover! Stapled! *You had to follow the schedule!*

And just after my parents left was some sort of "Meet Your Dorm" hoo-ha; I had, originally, uncurled myself and attended. Schedule!

Then I heard the following: "Okay, we want everyone to choose a partner."

And just as I was beginning to cringe, it sank in—

I didn't have to be here!

I. Did not. Have. To be. Here.

Who was going to check? Were they taking attendance? And what would they do if they discovered I wasn't there? Excommunicate me?

I didn't have to be here!

I slipped up the North tower steps a woman no staples could hold. My parents were gone. They had no idea what I was doing, who I was doing it with, and where. Or, in this case, not doing, with nobody, in *my room*.

I stood in the center of my tossed-about single room, hands on hips, the hallway outside nothing but layer on layer of silence. So. I could do whatever I wanted.

What would I do?

I would... *hang stuff up.*

I Sticky Tak-ed my way around the walls, slapping up a newspaper clipping here, a picture of my sister and me sitting on a huge ceramic lion there. Postcards of the Dome. A black and white picture of Boomer Esiason looking furious. A map of campus and a dot-matrix sign reading "SMC: Where Every Night is Ladies' Night" on the inside of my door.

And then—the knock.

I froze.

The knock came again, louder.

"Come in."

"It's locked."

I reached for the door. On the other side of it stood a tiny blonde who was not, as God had originally intended, a blonde. I bit my lip, trying to place her. The girl I'd accidentally flung Tater Tots on in the dining hall?

"Amy," she prompted. "I live next door?"

Ah. No wonder I didn't remember. I had met Amy fleetingly and under move-in conditions. Over the summer Saint Mary's, in her perpetual display of hospitality, had sent each member of the Class of '99 the home addresses of a corridormate. Go ahead! Write each other! Pre-borrow shoes!

This entire scenario had me twisting my hands for days. What do you write to a total stranger who for the next nine months will be sleeping, studying, and entertaining the opposite sex eight centimeters of plaster away?

I went through multiple drafts.

"Dear Amy—"

That got flushed. Too formal.

"Hi there!"

No. No. *That* was someone who dotted her i's with alternating smiley faces and hearts and walked the floor nights trying to

8

discern if *Beaches* or *Dirty Dancing* was her absolute, most favoritest movie in the whole wide world.

"*Hey*—"

Okay, now I sounded like someone in perpetual search of my babydaddy.

Finally I settled on:

> *Amy,*
>
> *Hi. My name's Mary Beth. We're going to be next-door neighbors at Saint Mary's. I certainly hope you don't have an obsession with knives! Well, gotta go. See you in August!*
>
> *Your next-door neighbor who does not have an obsession with knives, unless of course you do, in which case I'm completely okay with that,*
>
> *Mary Beth*
>
> *P.S. I wear a 7 ½.*

When I actually met the recipient of this masterpiece, it was amongst a morass of disgruntled family members and heavy boxes.

"I'm, um, Mary Beth. I wrote to you?" I said after I hesitantly traversed the two inches of hallway that separated us.

"Hi! You have atrocious handwriting!" she said.

I fled.

Now—three days later—she stood in my doorway, cradling half a dozen cans of powdered drink mixes.

"*Well?*"

I stood aside. "You wanna come in?"

She did, looking afraid when she saw the patchwork quilt my walls had become. "This... makes a statement," she finally said.

I kneaded a wad of Sticky Tak between my fingers, glancing around at my statement. It said: "I suck at life."

Amy noticed my red-rimmed eyes. "Your folks just leave?" I nodded. "Mine left yesterday," she said. "And when they got home they shipped me *this.*" She held out the canisters of Kool-Aid and Country Time.

"That's... nice..."

"No it *isn't*," she wailed. "It's *bizarre*. I never drink this stuff. I *hate* this stuff. *Look* at this. They sent me three different flavors of Crystal *Lite*. And they sent it ex*press,* like I was dying of thirst on a desert *island* or something. *Why*, Mary Beth?"

I stood silently, as yet unaware that every event in Amy's life warranted many italics.

She was frowning down at the Kool-Aid Man. "And *granola* bars. Good thing they sent *granola bars*, too. Which I *also* hate."

"Well! In any case, it's been very nice seeing you again, and—"

She grabbed my arm. "I *have* to *tell Edmonds.* Have you met Katie Edmonds in 219?"

Even after I said "Yes," she dug in four fingernails and dragged me down the hallway.

"Oh—I... left my door unlocked, and... the stereo on..."

"Edmonds! Edmonds! *Look* at what my idiot *parents* sent!"

An echoey response boomed down the hall. "I'M IN THE *SHOWER!*"

Amy pulled me into the bathroom and started rattling shower curtains. *"Ed*monds, ohmigod, you, like, *have* to *see*—" she screeched into the second stall.

"I'M OVER *HERE!"* Edmonds roared over the water.

We skittered across the tile to the opposite end of the bathroom.

"Edmonds, Edmonds. *Look* at this." Amy chucked a canister of pink lemonade over the shower curtain bar.

"OW! GOD! GOOD THING I'M SHAVING MY LEGS, YOU SOW!"

"With *my shave cream.* You *took* my shave cream."

"WHAT IS THIS, ANYWAY?"

"Friggin' *powdered drink mixes.* They sent me, like, *ninety million different kinds.*"

"KOOL-AID, TOO?"

"Yes."

"PRE-SUGARED?"

"Mostly," Amy said.

I heard a shampoo bottle bounce to the tile, immediately followed by a howled "SHIT!" And then: "EVEN, LIKE, THE MOUNTAIN BERRY FLAVOR?"

"I think so."

"CAN I HAVE IT?"

Amy cradled her vessels of sugar. "God! *God,* no, Edmonds, you wipe! My *parents* sent me these! *Express!* You think I'm such an ungrateful bitch that I hand around the stuff my *parents* send me? *Express?*"

The water stopped, the dripping of the shower head punctuated by a hearty "SKANK."

"You wanna meet Mary Beth?" said Amy.

I cleared my throat. "Hello, Edmonds."

There was a pause. *"WHO* IS THIS?"

"Room 212," Amy said.

"OH!" A wet bundle of white hair and a pair of drenched eyelashes peered out from behind the shower curtain. "ATROCIOUS HAND-WRITING GIRL! HI!" Edmonds waved, baptizing everything within an eight-foot radius.

Amy leapt out of the way. "Katie! Good thing you're *ruining* the shit my *mother* sent me."

"I'm very glad to meet you," I lied.

The shower curtain zipped back. Edmonds clomped out of the stall, an Anheuser-Busch towel wrapped around her, ducking under the curtain bar. "I'M FROM THE SOUTH SIDE OF SHECAAAAAHHHHHHH-GO," she announced. "YOU?"

"Cincinnati," Amy said. "Like, in *Ohio.*"

"ON PURPOSE?" Edmonds wanted to know.

"Where are the girls?" Amy asked. "The stupid partner thing they had going on downstairs is over."

"I'LL CHECK," Edmonds offered, picking up her shower tote while, as though it were humanly possible, raising her voice to holler, "GRACE! KATHY! PATTY!"

"I think I better—" I said, gesturing with my ball of Sticky-Tak.

"Oh, *no!*" Amy says, clamping on again. "You *have* to meet the *girls.*"

I backed closer to the door. "Listen, my CD player—"

She waved her hand around. "What *was* that crap you were playing? You can borrow my *Pulp Fiction* soundtrack. Make sure you give it back, though. Graceeeeeee!" she squeals. "So did he, like, *call?*"

Graceeeeeee had banged through the door. She had dark cropped hair and barely came up to Edmond's forearm. "Yes," she said, joining the talk show in the ladies' room. Another freshman trailed in after her.

"And did you pick up the phone?"

"No," Grace said.

Edmonds continued to stand there, dripping.

Amy nodded her approval. "Now he knows you're, like, *unattainable.* Guys *love* that. Look, my *parents* sent me—"

"Patty, come here," Grace said, huddling in the shower stall Katie just vacated. "I have to show you something."

Patty smiled at me. "I grew up in Columbus," she said. "Your door sign said you're from—"

"Did he call?" a disembodied voice screamed down the hall.

"Yes. I let the machine get it." Grace hollered back. Then lowered her voice and pointed to a spot on the floor next to her. "Stand right over here. You have to get really close." Patty obeyed, and Grace stomped in one of Edmond's puddles.

I inched closer to the door.

"Does anyone have movies?" Patty wanted to know, after she cupped a handful of water under the faucet and slung it in Grace's face.

"Mary Beth does," Amy volunteered. "I saw them."

The door slammed me in the left buttcheek. "Why are we all in the bathroom?"

"KATHY! KATHY, THIS IS MARY BETH. SHE HAS, LIKE, FOUR THOUSAND MOVIES AND SHE SAID WE CAN ALL WATCH THEM."

I pretended to test the soap dispenser. Now there was a "Kathy" to keep track of.

Kathy examined her contacts in the mirror. "For God's sake, Edmonds, put some clothes on."

Patty pointed at me. "Do you have *Top Gun?*"

Amy stacked her drink mixes in a pyramid. "Good idea. Let's go to MB's room."

"Oh, it's a mess," I said.

"He called," Grace said to Kathy.

"Who called?"

"That guy I met at the Notre Dame bookstore. I'm sorry, what's your name again? I think I sat next to you at that 'Meet The Dining Hall Staff' thing—"

"I'M IN THE MOOD FOR *THE PRINCESS BRIDE.* DO YOU HAVE *THE PRINCESS BRIDE?*" Edmonds wanted to know.

"The guy buying the astronomy textbook?"

"No, that's the *other* one. This is the one in my ROTC squadron."

"You're in ROTC?" Patty said.

"Wha'd he say?" Kathy wanted to know.

Grace frowned. "I don't know. I didn't *answer* the phone. You never *answer.*" She turned to Patty. "Yeah. Army."

"Do you have to wear a uniform to class?"

That was me.

I'd slipped around Amy's monument to Country Time and was halfway out the door. They stood facing me, Patty with her mascara half off, the Budweiser can-clad Edmonds, Grace standing in her damp socks, Kathy bracing one eye open with her thumb and index finger.

"Sometimes," Grace said.

I stretched out the Sticky-Tak; if I pressed it around my thumb long enough, the whorls of my fingerprint were left behind. "I have *The Princess Bride* if you want to borrow it, Katie."

She toasted me with her shower tote.

Amy held a canister up to the light. "*Look* at this. They sent me *caffeine free* iced tea."

Thaaaaaaaaaat was enough people-ing for one day. I darted out, letting the door of 212 swing shut behind me.

But I didn't lock it.

chapter three

Regina

I lived much of my freshman year in a state of suspension. I mean this literally. The hallways of my dorm were so narrow I used to plant my feet on one wall and my hands on the other, walk the walls to the ceiling, and hover. This was particularly useful when I wanted to hide, or think, or simply terrify. Ceiling tile is highly non-judgmental, I found, and did not care that I was eighteen years old and still awaiting my first date. While my corridormates walked oblivious beneath me, their words, their one AM radioactive energy, bounced off the walls and into my clothes as I hung there, absorbing.

If you and I were standing in front of Regina I would point at it and say, "In this building, I lay my head down every night for the happiest nine months of my life," and you would nod and ask where we found room for an open bar in there.

On the day I moved in, I carried with me the following:

A box marked "Special Occasion Bras"
My entire Jimmy Buffett collection
A powder blue wastebasket crammed full of shoes, toe of a red
    cowboy boot peering over the top
A Ziplock bag containing seven animal cookies. Icing: Pink.
Four garbage bags labeled "Not Garbage." These held towels,

sheets, pillows, pillowcases, a bedspread, and stuffed purple mouse named Squeaky.

A tiny, tiny television set, to which was duct-taped a tiny, tiny remote control. Move-In Day was the last time they were together in this world; after the tape was removed, the remote was sucked into an alternate—indubitably larger—universe and has yet to be seen again. I hail thee from afar, remote.

A map of the Grand Canyon

A mini-refrigerator, hauled up two flights of steps by my pending brother-in-law, stuffed to the tip of its wee icebox with a four-month supply of Always Pantiliners. He did not know about the pantiliners.

This was the first load.

I highly doubted this was going down at the men's dorms across the street. Men can fit their entire existences into a duffel bag with room left over for a world-ending speaker system and the two slivers of Irish Spring which will serve as a universal cleaning agent. The average college-age male sees no need to coordinate the squalor in which he lives; high décor for him is a WonderBra ad and a neon beer sign facing the nearest administration building. The rest came courtesy of the dorm dumpster at the close of the previous semester.

When I made my campus visit, my hostesses shuttled me across the street to the dorm room of two of their male Notre Dame friends. They met us in the lobby, bouncing on their toes. "Hi! Guess what!" they said. "We got a *table!*"

I followed them as they took the stairs two at a time to their room. Well! A *table!* I scornfully reflected upon my brother-in-law's college apartment, the living room of which featured fourteen chairs of varying make and model, all reverently angled towards the nineteen-inch television set in the corner, and a one-eyed deer head with cigarettes jammed up both nostrils. *These* guys had a table. Possibly even lampshades!

And my future brothers proudly flung open the door of their

room to reveal: an ironing board balanced across two cement blocks. "Sweet, right?" one said, slapping it with a fraternal metallic clatter. Rust flakes fluttered to the twelve-pack boxes stacked below.

Women, on the other hand, parachute into new homes armed with photo montages and stuffed animals and bathmats, all of which must match the sheets, the liquid soap dispenser, the throw pillows, and the duvet cover. We pack wee little hardback books with inch-long pages that only delicate female fingers can turn. And female college freshmen, many of whom are in control of their surroundings for the very first time, don't just feather the nest... they sponge paint the twigs an adorable shade of dusty rose. *This* is civilized.

Where Regina is featured on the Saint Mary's College website, it is photographed from very, very far away. I lived in Regina's North tower, and by "tower" I mean "wide rectangular...thing." It was constructed in the 1960's, the height of the Age of Public Ugly, and like nearly every large building of the era is boring and identical in all directions.

The rooms were eight feet by twelve feet.

In those days, Regina housed a basement lounge where old, sad furniture went to die. Orange vinyl chairs and brown nappy couches and avocado tabletops: This was a social space that also doubled as a living testament to the prevailing tastes of the Carter administration.

The first floor had a chapel, a post-Vatican II affair with metal fish for door handles and the occasional potted palm tree. We worshipped a groovy sort of Lord, there in Regina Hall.

Regina also hostessed the campus pool, which I found exciting until the day the hall council abruptly cancelled an all-school pool party the day it was to take place. This caused a minor uproar.

I caught my RA in the hall and demanded answers.

"What is this? I think we deserve to know. If the administration of this school is—"

"Somebody threw up in the pool," she said.

You did what you could, in Regina. The upperclassmen in the

other dorms had huge windows and walk-in closets and space to spin. You, Freshman, had one washer and dryer per floor and walls that were more of a permeable membrane than a soundproof barrier. But you pillowed yourself with Squeaky and the Grand Canyon and a till-menopause supply of feminine products.

You planted your feet and you hung in there.

chapter four
✳ ✳ ✳

Security

At a women's college, you live in lockdown.

Our dorms were bolted and alarmed and guarded like East Berlin. This was a matter of security, and also smugness. Men were... not welcome in the dorms. All males of the species were to be escorted through the halls, even dads, even to the bathroom, and they weren't permitted past the bell desk until we deigned to fetch them. Friday and Saturday nights were rife with clots of Domers using the single landline at the bell desk—this was before cell phones, if you can imagine the Earth as such; I believe the Appalachian foothills had just been created—and they had to sit and wait for us to make a grand entrance. This, I felt, was the ultimate feminist statement.

But the men's dorms at our brother school played host to all the parties, seeing as they offered the same level of security as your average convenience store with an anti-theft system consisting entirely of a mirror mounted on the ceiling. Notre Dame's women's halls were shackled up as much as ours were.

Saint Mary's security system extended to the infrastructure of the dorms. Four years of my life were largely spent roped to my room key and student ID card. Saint Mary's residence halls were rigged with a "detex" system that kept the doors locked until we ran our cards through a little box mounted on the door frames. The first time I tried to detex, I whipped my card out, deftly inserted it in the scanner, and firmly tugged on the handle of... a still-locked door.

Well—crap.

Repeat.

Crap.

Repeat.

By this time there was a line of freshmen behind me patiently waiting to proceed into the dorm. I tried again. *(Crap.)* "I think there's something wrong with my ID," I said to the girl behind me.

"Or," she said, "you could try not running it through upside-down."

I considered this, until one of our classmates exited through the other side. The lot of us grabbed the door before it swung shut and walked on through.

chapter five

＊ ＊ ＊

Rah

Unlike most of my classmates, my first brush with Notre Dame worship came not at my father's knee or through a Saint Mary's or Notre Dame education vicariously experienced through an older sibling. It came my junior year of high school, when my U.S. history teacher, who otherwise gave the impression that he was a fairly sane human being, sat us all down in the first semester and announced that we would be awarded extra points on our test grades each time Notre Dame emerged victorious. When they won the national championship, he finished dramatically, one point would be added to our quarter grade.

The Class of '95 suddenly became very, very concerned about the Saturday fates of the Irish.

One girl raised her hand. "What if they lose a game?"

He stared at her. "They won't *lose*," he said.

The shift in allegiances was bothersome. I was a Bengals fan before I could even find Notre Dame on a map with binoculars and a global positioning satellite, so when I gained admittance to Saint Mary's, I tread worrisomely over the whole issue of how I was now supposed to feel about Joe Montana. He took the Super Bowl away from my team! But now he was my brother in the Notre Dame family! But he made Boomer Esiason cry! But he helped win the Cotton Bowl the year I was born!

To crash course, I found Lou Holtz's account of Notre Dame's 1988 championship season, and sat and underlined what I was supposed to do at the football games. It seemed to involve a great deal of weeping and arm-waving. I could expect a band and an Irish Guard and great hoards of people, and as I read this, sitting in my father's office as I worked the phone lines the summer before I was to report to Saint Mary's, I shook in the face of being a part of this. I honestly did. I turned the pages and trembled.

I didn't get out much.

The concept of this thing known as a "pep rally" was entirely foreign to me. Pep rallies at my high school consisted of the student body imprisoned in the gym at eighth bell to generate bored applause for the golf team while a band borrowed from one of the local all-male schools attempted "Louie Louie" in the background, and so, with this as my frame of reference, I wasn't planning on attending any of Notre Dame's. This horrified Justine, who, as a sophomore, already had a whole entire football season to show for her advanced age.

"You're not going to the first rally?" she asked in the same tones one might use to say something along the lines of, "The primary component of the air you breathe isn't oxygen?"

At that particular moment she was arranging a coffee maker on top of her toaster oven. Justine's single was decorated in Early Delinquent. If the College had decreed it illegal to own, it could be found, discreetly sheeted, beneath her loft. Candles, a popcorn popper, hot plate: If you wanted to die a fiery death, you would do well to spend the night in Justine's room.

"You *need* to go to at least one," she said. "Fondue party in my room before we leave."

Amy brought the drinks.

So the evening before the first home game of the season, I tagged along with my corridormates, obscenely early for seating purposes, to the Joyce Athletic and Convocation Center at our brother school. Kickoff for the game against Northwestern was a good sixteen hours away, and the entire Vatican had descended upon campus.

The students were crammed way, way up in the cheap seats, a screaming drunk hormonal mass of raw collegiate pep, flasks and frequent trips to the bathroom in every direction.

Across from the bleacher onto which Two North had squeezed itself—we had to stand sideways—was a glaring, solid rectangle of red T-shirts. These, Justine informed us, were the men of Zahm Hall, and we were supposed to disdain them mightily, as far as I could tell because they took it upon themselves to lead rally cheers until the Notre Dame Marching Band showed up.

I struggled to discern words, beats, cadences, a difficult feat in the acoustical River of Death that is a basketball arena. Zahm succeeded in cheerleading until the clapping got out of rhythm, which, in an arenafull of white Catholics, was quite within seconds.

Zahm eventually became bored with the chanting and clapping and started the Wave, which amused the drunks for a while. We congratulated ourselves with great ovations whenever the Wave made a complete lap of the arena; in South Bend, Indiana, on a Friday night, this was about as close to entertainment as any of us were going to get.

At seven-thirty a tiny, tiny figure, supported by much slurred screeching, ran to the center of the basketball court.

Edmonds slapped my arm. "THE LEPRECHAUN!" she screamed in my ear.

He attacked the podium, a sole bearded figure before a sea of empty folding chairs on the floor and full-to-bursting bleachers in the nosebleed sections. "WELCOME TO THE 1995 FOOTBALL SEASON!"

The fact that the world had not ended between the end of last season and that evening was greatly applauded.

Notre Dame's Marching Band streamed onto the floor, blasting the Victory March. I danced along as well as a grace-impaired person hemmed in on all sides by corridormates could dance. Somebody fell off the edge of our bleacher, in time, it should be noted, to the music.

The last raging notes had barely been swallowed into the cinderblock when the arena lights are dimmed. "HEY!" a voice behind us yelled. "It's DARK!"

An ovation was made to the absence of light.

Said the Leprechaun: "And NOW," ("WOOOOOOOOOO!" screamed a lone voice behind me. We *loved* "NOW!") "LAdies and GENTLEmen" (another howl from the general direction of Zahm), "please WELCOME..." (final, almost unbearable dramatic pause) *"YOUR FIGHTING IRISH!"*

Victory March. Swirling spotlights. Row upon row of football players wearing suits crowding into the folding chairs. The 1956 Republican Convention goes to a pep rally.

Following the Parade of Athletes came speeches from former players and current players, the main themes of which seemed to be as follows:

1. Northwestern is Not ND. Northwestern sucks.

2. But we *are* ND;

3. so we don't.

Following each speaker scattered students howled "Lou! Loo-ouuuu!" into the otherwise polite cheering, holding up spread-apart thumbs and index fingers.

"I'm gonna bring out The Man now," the Leprechaun said at one point, and I flung my arms in the air.

"REGIS!" I screamed.

Anne hit me. "Lou *Holtz*."

The Band struck up the last few bars of the "1812 Overture", and between rests we brought our "L"s down to shoulder level, then raised them again. "Lou!" we said. "Lou!" This was the high-coordination point of the evening.

For a person at least as popular around campus as Jesus Christ, Lou Holtz was surprisingly short. Perhaps, however, this is because I was looking down on him from an altitude normally reserved for commercial jets.

He spoke. He was simple, humble, honest, and when he was done being simple, humble and honest he said, "I want you to put your arms around the person on your right and the person on your left, and sing to your school and Mother, Notre Dame."

The Band wound into the Alma Mater. The drunks slammed into one another. Zahm wept. The cheerleaders formed what passed for a straight line.

Two North hesitated.

I knew the words, but am entirely unsure as to whether I was allowed to sing them. So, wary of stepping on Domer toes, we hung back when the swaying started. Then Amy dug her elbow into my side and indicated the male swaying partner to her left, who had one arm around the female Domer to his right and had slung the other across Amy's shoulder, hand dangling on the upper regions of her bra strap.

We fell in.

chapter six

✳ ✳ ✳

Things to do Between Weekends

H*istorty of Western Civilization*
I minored in U.S. history, because to major in history would mean many classes about the development of people other than myself, and this was boring. With a minor, however, I could specialize in the wonder and glory of the nation that had produced the wonderful and glorious eighteen-year-old meeeeeeee.

I still had to take a whole year of The History of Western Civilization, the textbook for which weighed one million pounds and contained an entire chapter entitled "The Development of the Hand-Plow."

The most important moment in The History of Western Civilization occurred on October 3, 1995. Class convened at the exact moment when the verdict of the O.J. Simpson murder trial was to come down. We showed up early and asked our professor if he would cancel class so we could hear the reading, but he said no, we were going to have a lecture on Constantine, who, he said, was the first Roman Emperor to ban the abduction of young women, and really was a jolly sort of fellow, as emperors go, and we were expected to discuss all of this, in detail, on the homework assignment, so *sit down*.

The professor did, however, permit two students to go to his office and listen to the reading on the radio. They fled, and we sat and not-listened about Constantinople until we heard the following ricochet down the hall:

"OHHHHHHHHHHHHHHHHHH!"

The missing two slammed back into the classroom, one flopping dramatically into her desk: *"Not guilty!"*

There was a brief onset of pandemonium, and then we mopped up the angst and entrails we'd spattered on the classroom walls and went back to the far less compelling Constantine, who, after all, never rushed for two thousand yards.

Every Single English Class, Ever

Because it was my primary major (political science was the other one, and that degree pretty much only comes in useful once every four years, so check back with me later on when nobody understands the electoral college again), Saint Mary's was the only college I'd looked at that offered a BA in English writing, which effectively combined the traditional uselessness of an English major with all the unhirability of a degree in creative writing.

The English writing emphasis, however, did not excuse me from the occasional lit class. I was exposed to a great many of these, and for the most part they were genre-based. I will now save you four years:

Drama: Somebody dies.

Comedy: Somebody dies, but you're supposed to laugh about it.

Plays Written By People Too Unimaginative to Come Up With a Plot of Their Own, So They Stole One From a Book Somebody Else Has Already Written: May involve characters that have already died in the book.

Musicals: Somebody dies of too much choreography, and then everybody else sings about it.

In the writing courses, we wrote essays and short stories four seconds before they were due, and handed them around, and everybody would sip coffee and nod slowly and say things like,

"Oh… the *voice.*" This was excellent preparation for graduate school.

Spanish

Spanish spoken by a learned or native tongue is lovely. Spanish spoken by a hungover eighteen-year-old at nine in the morning is not.

Spanish and I might have gotten along had the text met my academic needs. What I needed was a book with realistic learning goals, clearly written explanations, and illustrations in which the people did not look like natives of the planet Tooltron. What I got was *¡Dímelo tú!*

¡Dímelo tú!, which from what I can figure (the book never said, exactly) may be translated as, "¡You Will Fail!", was a foreign horror film in textbook form. It taught via the immersion method, which plunges the student directly into full use of the language, assuming he will suddenly and miraculously catch on and form the ability to order tortillas with a side of early Argentinean poetry by noon. This is akin to installing in the cockpit of the space shuttle a person whose concept of flying does not extend beyond beverage service in coach: "Let's try slowing our orbit so we can re-enter the atmosphere. Go ahead, play around with the stick a little. You'll get a feel for it."

So in order to lull us into a false sense of security, everything in *¡Dímelo tú!* was in English for the first four pages of Chapter One, and then the authors, assured that we had completely mastered the language by now, proceeded to write everything—explanations, exercise directions, photo captions, evvvvvverything—in Spanish. And Chapter One didn't start us off with a few useful throwaway phrases like "Excuse me" or "Good morning" or "I would like a beverage containing large amounts of alcohol, please." No. Chapter One—Chapter ONE—contained the following:

Subject pronouns
An introduction to the irregular verb *ser*

All about articles and nouns
One hundred and twenty-five vocabulary words
   (I *counted them.*)
Singular forms of adjectives
Present tense of verbs ending in -ar
An introduction to the irregular verb *ir*

Spanish appeared in my life at 9 AM four days a week, earlier and more often than any other class, not counting our required one hour per week locked up in the Language Lab.

Language Lab was the Foreign Language Department's attempt at "interactive learning" and involved us sitting at little cubicles with tape decks, listening to exercises in our respective languages. To ensure that we didn't merely sign in for our time and then escape, our student ID's, our lives, were taken at the door and returned to us when we signed out. We were to listen carefully to incomprehensible passages in Spanish, repeat them, then answer equally incomprehensible questions concerning said passages in a workbook.

This learning strategy succeeded for maybe one hour of the twenty we had to spend under classroom arrest, all of us hunching over our cubicles and correctly pronouncing maybe the first word of the sentence we were supposed to be repeating, then following it by a muttered mishmash of vaguely Latin-based syllables.

Then somebody realized that the workbook had all the answers in the back, and as long as you wore your headset and had a tape in the deck the student proctor assumed you were interacting away. So we'd show up for our Language Lab time with our Hootie and the Blowfish mixes and homework for other classes hidden within our wonderful workbooks, prepared for yet another exciting episode of *¡Dímelo tú Hates You!*

By October, my primary strategy in the face of this was to cram together the little I remembered of my high school French and stick an "o" on the end of every other word. This largely didn't work, perhaps because I was making such productive use of my Language

Lab time. *¡Dímelo tú!* forged on.

Years later, I sat in graduation exercises in a polyester robe and a tassly hat with my *magna cum laude* diploma resting on my lap, wondering how I'd so narrowly missed *summa*. Which was the one class that bumped me down? Advanced U.S. Public Policy? Medieval Literature? Aerobics?

Suddenly I realized...it was the one D—the *one*—I'd ever gathered in my entire life.

Screw you, *¡Dímelo tú!*

Victorian Literature

This is what I took home from Victorian Literature:

1. Oscar Wilde? Gay.

Philo/Theo

I signed up for a "tandem course" as a freshman, which sounds carnal and slightly dangerous but is actually a pretentious way of saying "three hours long." We took theology and philosophy back-to-back, with two profs and intertwining material. First the philosophy guy told us that "The Little Engine That Could" was a bunch of crap, and this all had to do with Socrates, or something; and everybody got mad at him; and then the theology guy gave us "The Lion, the Witch and the Wardrobe" and told us it was actually a Christian parable and not about wardrobes at all, and everybody got mad at him.

They *wanted* us mad at them. Philosophy Guy—who asked us to call him "Kevin", which severely deflated my view of the discipline, because... Aristotle, Plato, Aquinas, and *Kevin*—anyway, Kevin would perch on the edge of his desk and say, "Good! Anybody else?" when we announced to him that he was, in fact, a poopyhead.

"Contrary to what you've likely been told your entire lives, I'm sorry to inform you that we can't all be right," he beamed at us on Day One. "If you want an A in this course, we are going to expect you to be as judgmental as hell." We all took careful notes when he said this, and then both profs laughed at us and called us freshmen, because we did not yet understand that you weren't supposed to write anything down unless it was first prefaced by "Now, this is going to be on the test."

The theology guy, for his part—he told us to call him Joe, and gave us his home phone number on the condition that we promised to never call him when *Seinfeld* was on—was all hot and bothered about this new... thing. It was a computer thing, and what you did was type messages and send them back and forth, even to a lot of people at once.

"Email," he said.

"So you want us to... have a discussion by computer?'

"Yes."

"But can't we do that... in here? During class?"

"Well—yeah. But with *this*, you use the *computer.* Isn't that great?"

That *was* great, as far as I was concerned, seeing as it didn't involve actual people. It was the first course in the history of Saint Mary's to do such a thing. This was in the days of pizza-dimensioned floppy disks, when hard drives were the size of battleships and held maybe 4k, the College's server was located in a hashish lab in upper Oregon, and my email address was something like ellis.mary.beth@saintmarys.1811.pine.net.edu. Amy and Carah were also in the tandem, and we would sit scowlingly in the Greg Brady Memorial Lounge in the basement of Regina to await our turn to do our homework on one of the five monochrome screens.

We were also encouraged to turn in our course assignments in typed format, which allowed me to develop the vital academic skill of transforming a five-page paper into a seven-page one simply by changing the font.

The computer, however, could work against us. Many of us discovered this amazing thing called a "spellcheck," and what was great about the spellcheck was, it would change stuff *for* you. You didn't have to do—or *know*, even—*anything!*

One day we handed in carefully formatted essays on Blase Pascal's *Pensées*, and we all agreed that he was very Pascally, all right, and then Joe cleared his throat and said, "I'm going to ask you ladies to please take care with the spell check. Sometimes, you know, it replaces what the computer thinks is a misspelled word, and the correction is spelled properly, but it might not be the word you want."

What did he mean?

He refused to elaborate.

One of our classmates inched a hand into the air: Celeste. "I... think I know what he's talking about," she said.

The tandem had a reunion just before we graduated, and we agreed that we didn't remember much of anything from freshmen classes except being judgmental as hell, and then Celeste walked in and we all asked her how Pascal's penises were doing.

Gender in Politics

I wrote a paper on the women's movement in Iran. Title: "Women As a Windsock."

Math

I slid into Saint Mary's on the strength of my high school GPA and admission essay, which, upon asked to address "a major life question with which you have been struggling," I entitled "Why Did You Bother Asking What My Gender Is On The Application?"

What almost stopped me were my SAT scores. The SAT purports to predict how well a high school student will do in college. According to the SAT, I would be fortunate to reason my way out of the building in which I was currently taking the test.

In order to knock out my freshman math requirement, I tried to enroll in "The Language of Math", which was the most basic math class you could take at Saint Mary's without dropping to an assist from Big Bird. You had to get special permission to get in, sort of like an honors class for the spatially challenged.

But the Freshman Office took one look at my miraculous feat of graduating in the top ten percent of my high school class and ruled me able to hack through "Liberal Arts Mathematics." I pointed out that the main reason I was able to achieve such a high class rank was because I hadn't signed up for any math my senior year and took a remedial course in algebra as a junior, sitting between a freshman and a girl who licked eraser shavings off her desk.

"Look at your geometry grade. You got a B."

"I can *do* geometry! All you do is count lines in geometry!"

"Mary Beth—really. In American society it's considered acceptable for women to say they struggle with math, but you're not going to get away with that at Saint Mary's."

"I AM AN ENGLISH MAJOR!"

I was given an Orientation-sounding speech about Needing a Challenge and sent forth to expand my mind.

Well... perhaps I was underestimating myself, anyway. I had survived high school algebra; I would survive Liberal Arts Mathematics.

I lasted maybe one sixteenth of one class. Could be more. Could be less. It is beyond my capacity to fraction it out for you.

I should have known what I was in for when I looked up the prof's name on the syllabus and saw that it was about three inches long and contained no vowels. I could pretty much make out what he was saying until he grabbed a piece of chalk and put a horrifying "sample problem" on the board involving quadrants and graphs and moving trains and I don't know what-all and I ran, very fast, back to the Freshman Office.

I sought out my counselor and cried a little and begged a lot; then I noticed the folder open on the desk in front of her. "Is that my application file?" She nodded. "Pull my SAT scores."

"I really don't see what—"

"*Pull* the *num*bers."

She looked at me, back at the scores, then back at me again.

The SAT had worked for me at last. "See?" I said. "Ninety-seventh percentile in verbal abilities, and *fifth* percentile in math." I said this last part with immense pride, as if announcing that I had in fact received an Olympic gold medal instead of scoring lower than ninety-five percent of every single student who had taken the test world-wide that year.

"I've never seen a disparity quite so... dramatic."

"That's *right.*"

She actually called in one of the instructors of Math 101. "I want you to meet Mary Beth," the counselor said. "She's a very... interesting student." This was administrator-ese for: "Lookit the freak."

My SAT scores were produced, with the same amount of throat-clearing and raised eyebrows. Finally the prof folded her hands in her lap.

"Sometimes," she said delicately, "students just learn math differently. I don't see why this young lady should continue beating her head against a brick wall if Math 101 can help her find a way over it."

She smiled at me. "We write essays."

I passed Math 101.

✳ ✳ ✳

As a senior, I took a course for students considering teaching at the college level. We spent some time on learning disabilities, and discussed one recently isolated by psychologists and educational specialists.

Symptoms include struggling with basic mathematical concepts and application of formulas, often paired with a predilection for the language arts and the odd ability to perform well in geometry. It's called dyscalculia.

Shakespeare For the English Major

This was high-octane stuff, I'll have you know. We skipped *Romeo and Juliet* and shot straight into *King Lear.* The course was taught by a kindly, enormously educated Sister of the Holy Cross who probably came with the College when it was founded in 1844. She was about four feet tall and read monologues in a dulcet rasp, and once she brought us a lovely tea and spent ten minutes arranging the sugar packets in a decorative pink fan.

The class was performance-based, heavy on character study and word play. We felt sorry for Richard III for about two acts, and then we hated him again. There then followed weeks and weeks of *Hamlet*, which unfolded in a properly staid Danish fashion, and then we got to Act III, Scene II, and none of us have been quite right since.

"Now, girls," said the good sister, "let's look at this dialogue between Hamlet and Ophelia. He says, 'Lady, shall I lie in your lap?' and she refuses. He then says, 'Do you think I meant country matters?'"

She removed her glasses. "Who can discuss for us the import of this? Anyone?"

We sat silently, staring at her.

"Hamlet was crudely insulting Ophelia, girls. He was referring, of course, to the cunt. Ophelia's *vagina*."

I blacked out everything concerning Shakespeare For the English Major after that.

Biology

Saint Mary's had a two-semester lab requirement, even for the arts and letters majors, which meant I had to choose between physics, chemistry, and biology. I picked the one with the text that seemed to rule by fear the least, and when I got to the front of the line in the bookstore the clerk said, "Oh—bio. You'll need your lab equipment." Whereupon she reached beneath the counter and presented me with a full-color, laminated picture of the innards of a fetal pig.

I had to take apart a squid in high school, which wasn't too bad, for in western Cincinnati, we rarely sat down to a hearty meal of it. Because we ate ham instead.

So the primary lesson I took away from bio was involuntary vomit control, which actually came in handy once I turned twenty-one. The lab final consisted of many stations of spread and pinned pigs, microscopes trained on various portions we were to cold-identify. I studied my pig picture while flying back and forth for

Thanksgiving break, even during the meal service, no doubt raising the following questions amongst the passengers sitting in my row:

1. Wha—?
2. Why are they letting her sit next to the emergency exit?

You know, somebody can *tell* you that you're going to see four long tables packed with dead baby pigs, but it doesn't really prepare you for the reality of the thing. If I had needed any reason to remain an English major, it was now spread out before me.

At my first station I leaned over the eyepiece of the microscope and saw: a pink blur. I flagged down the prof, who took a glance, shrieked, adjusted the focus, and gave the pig a final refresher spritz of formaldehyde, forever preserving the front of my sweatshirt and about four blue books in the process.

As it happens, formaldehyde is not a good thing to smell when you're nervous at eight o'clock in the morning.

In the second semester, now that we'd established that dead pigs tend to stay put, we studied animal response. We spent several weeks with male beta fighting fish, scientifically illustrating that when you hold up little colored squares of construction paper next to the bowl, the fish will spaz out and you get to laugh and laugh.

We were permitted to bring our test subjects to the dorms with us for three dollars, and a few days after I brought home my new friend, whom I christened Patton Schwarzkopf, I developed a case of hurts-to-circulate-white-blood-cells, beg-for-the-Rapture bronchitis. (I strongly suspect the fish had something to do with this.) It was the first time I had been sick and away from my mother's cool washcloths for my forehead, and I was calling home with hourly updates on current Phlegm Conditions.

At one point I managed to climb the ladder of my loft, an act that required about twenty minutes per rung. When I at last reached my mattress, I passed out, oblivious to a fire drill, an hour-long serenade from my alarm clock radio, and Amy banging on my door screaming at me to turn down that country western hick music, for God's sake. When I did regain consciousness, it was about noon. I had slept through two classes and was well on my way to missing a third.

I said a four-letter word. I said lots of four-letter words. I had a different obscenity for each rung of the ladder. When I reached the ground, I doubled-checked the alarm clock on my desk and happened to notice the fish bowl—the empty fish bowl—sitting next to it.

Oh...no.

I recoiled against the loft. For my fish to commit suicide was one thing, but for him to commit it all over my homework was quite another.

I clenched my teeth and picked up the looseleaf page, holding it at arm's length and looking everywhere but at my crispy beta fish. With terrific bronchitis speed that reached upwards of a millimeter an hour, I headed for the corridor bathroom to give Patton Schwarzkopf a proper military burial at sea.

The Spanish essay, I turned in as-was.

chapter seven

Squadron Dance Maneuver

There were two opportunities to socialize as a freshman at Saint Mary's: You could go to a dorm party, and drink until you threw up, or you could go to a dance, and wear a pretty dress, and drink until you threw up on glitter.

At the dorm parties, approximately eighty percent of the under-21 population of Saint Mary's and Notre Dame stuffed themselves into a room designed to hold, on an inhale, maybe two people. The beer and the liquor flowed like Niagara Falls, only faster. We got away with this because Notre Dame had this firm, comprehensive alcohol policy, which at the time stated, and I quote, "The University will enter a private residence room for the purpose of enforcing Indiana law if drinking in such a room becomes public in any way."

The loophole word here is *public*—it was not incredibly wise, legally, to mess with the search and seizure rights of a student whose father had most likely graduated from Notre Dame's law school.

The style of dorm parties were cramped only by parietals. These were circumnavigated, however, by socializing in the hideously furnished "twenty four hour lounges", where anyone could be at any time. The only problem with the twenty four hour lounges was, in the women's dorms at least, that they were strategically placed in the high-traffic vicinity of the bell desk, at which sat a deceivingly benign-looking matron with a penchant for watching Andy Griffith reruns at high volumes, effectively creating an atmosphere about as charming as the county morgue.

Dances were all-age events and infinitely more stressful than parties. There were roughly five thousand dances per dorm per semester. Individual classes and clubs hosted them as well, thereby rendering the pool of dates who weren't previously spoken for, who adhered to rules of basic personal hygiene, and appeared to be planetary natives a fairly shallow one. At the height of dance season—which started immediately after football season ended and ran right up to finals week—nearly all the water had drained from the children's plastic wading pool.

Outside of the sparkling conversation they often generate, you could easily pick out a couple headed for an SYR from quads away, because *everybody dresses alike.* Dance nights turned the campus into a Catholic Twilight Zone, with the women in short black dresses with heels and the gentlemen in khaki pants and a navy blue blazer. You started to expect the football team to run out of the stadium tunnel dressed as such on game day. It was simply What Was Done, this business of the men of the University of Notre Dame dressing for romance like some sort of army on a Squadron Dance Maneuver.

I think we can trace this phenomenon back to the fact that a large percentage of the Notre Dame and Saint Mary's student body spent twelve years in Catholic school uniforms, and never quite lost the uneasy feeling that unless we all look like each other, someone is going to get slapped with a detention. Perhaps that's why dancing and drinking went hand-in-hand in South Bend—after a few you tended not to notice that your date, your roommate's date, and in fact everybody's date looked as if they had been ordered directly from an L.L. Bean catalogue.

I backed away from all of this in my first semester, which completely mystified Two North. I didn't drink, primarily because I was a classic thrower-upper and preferred not to pay the campus' practically official fake ID provider—he pretty much set up a booth with his gigantic lifesize license background at the Services Fair during Orientation—for the privilege. (Fake ID Guy had the ability to produce false driver's licenses from two states, Wisconsin and Iowa. You got to pick. On Friday nights 98% of the freshman class was from Des Moines.)

This relegated my social life to pretty much checking out the stock changes in the Saint Mary's Library vending machines ("You *guys!* They got in Hershey bars *with almonds!*")

But I didn't give my friends full disclosure, which was that the reason I shied away from major campus social events was because they involved interaction with the opposite sex, and *that* would *never* do. I grew up with girls, went to school with girls, ate with girls, whiffed at soccer balls each autumn with girls. Most of my teachers were grown-up girls. Boys were things to be avoided and, later, things to be feared. They were enjoyable to view at a minimum distance of eight or twelve feet—preferably behind some sort of barrier, not unlike a museum or zoo exhibit.

This attitude, I believe, may be directly attributed to Ken dolls. Between the two of us, my sister and I owned enough Barbies to populate a Naval base, but the Ken census topped out at about three. Ken's major feature was you could pop off his head with disturbing ease, leaving a tanned, well-muscled chest with a gaping neck hole. This opened the door for several creative Barbie-and-Ken story lines, among them "Ken Is the Victim of a Freak Farm Implement Accident," "Ken Gets a Job at the Local Alligator Farm," and "Ken Overcomes a Bizarre, As-Yet Unexplained Birth Defect." So my Ken's head was often missing from his body, his vacant, Baywatch smile tossed into my Barbie clothes trunk to mingle with the tiny high-heeled shoes and evening gowns.

This made me feel empowered, somehow, compensating for the fact that Barbie could not free-stand on thick carpeting—possibly due to the shape of her feet, which curved from toe to heel at an angle of ninety degrees. I was ten before I figured out that the main biological difference between women and men is not that men are the ones with the detachable necks.

"Walking problems with nice pecs," I would say when Two North attempted to set me up. I had certain ground rules, and the following candidates were pre-refused anyway:

Hair longer than mine
Hair dyed a primary color
Any part of the body voluntarily punctured
Even if it was a tasteful tattoo involving my name
Especially if it was a tasteful tattoo involving my name
Was under the impression that Dante Alighieri was
    some sort of pasta

Since this eliminated pretty much everybody not in Olympic training or en route to the seminary, this kept Two North busy searching and failing to ask why I always ran to Clorox the corridor whenever somebody's boyfriend walked past.

For a while.

chapter eight

* * *

Notes

At my first voice lesson as a college student, my teacher told me, within ten seconds of shaking my hand hello, that I needed to "drink water until the pee is clear."

It was a doomed relationship. At the year-end recital, I absolutely destroyed my semester grade by forgetting the second line of the second stanza to "The Rose." I feel this was a mental act of self-defense, the brain vomiting the song right back up at me so as not to be contaminated with the likes of "I say love it is a flower, and you its only seed."

Evil irony, for I am a second soprano. We sing beneath the first sopranos, who get the dog-calling, upper-end notes, and above the altos, who do a lot of "ba-bum"ing beneath the melody. I love singing second.

If only I didn't sound like a very angry wombat with a sinus infection.

I tried, at Saint Mary's, having discovered female choral singing at my sister's high school concerts. I tagged along with my mother to pick her up from a late rehearsal one afternoon, and echoing down the hall was two-part a cappella. I laid my miserable sixth-grade head against the doors, then slid inside and sat in the back of the theatre. The alto and the soprano melted into the musty air—this was a bunch of fourteen and fifteen year olds slogging through

"Alexander's Ragtime Band," and they very likely sucked, but the harmony slid over me, warm caramel. Surely, I thought, hands clenched in the skirt of my wrinkled grade school uniform, there was no lovelier sound on the face of the Earth than this.

I auditioned for—and clearly because few others had was admitted to—the World's Most Obviously Named Vocal Group, the Saint Mary's College Women's Choir. Few songs were in English, and there were no showtunes, which seemed to be the rule for Serious Music. This was something of a surprise, as the top choir at my high school rarely let a syllable drop without an assist from Rogers and Hammerstein. The Women's Choir sang "The Belles of Saint Mary's" and "The Magnificat," and we weren't allowed to wave at our friends in the audience and we never ever had hand motions, and I relaxed into the notion that few truly elite vocal ensembles throw synchronized shoulder rolls into every blasted thing.

But I didn't mind, because I didn't need to comprehend what we were singing to understand that the human voice, when properly struck against another human voice, provides a glorious sense of tonal smugness. Screw you, piano and trombone! Look what *we* can do! Sometimes during rehearsals the director would sustain us in the middle of a note, arms raised: Hold it hold it holllllllllllld it.... and the thick female braid of sound wound about the room.

And sometimes we were placed in a circle to check our pitch against the other vocal parts. The director stood imperiously in the center, keeping time, slowly spinning, stopping before offending off-key singers. When she pointed at me—and she always did— I cringed into my sheet music and stopped singing, camouflaging my English major's voice by mouthing the syllables. As she nod-ded at my sudden competence, I waited for her to move on to some other poor girl who had been in the bathroom when the Vocal Talent Fairy rang her doorbell. But she always circled right back to me. The voice lessons aided me in forming a water addiction but not much else.

In the audition I was asked to sight-read as another choir member played the piano.

This went every bit as well as you might expect. "Where... *are* you?" I said to the director as the accompanist banged away.

"Fourth measure."

I flipped pages.

"On page two."

I flipped some more.

"In the *soprano section.*"

So I faked it. During rehearsal I listened carefully to the far more capable women singing around me, I memorized the melody the seconds were in charge of, and I faked it. I had no control over how fast the music was or where the syllables went, and if I didn't figure out a way to get us all through this, somebody might find out that often I stared down at sheet music blurred by tears, thrilled at the rehearsal and yet desperately unable to keep up with it. So I plowed forward, answering the sopranos, layering with the altos, lost lost lost.

The Women's Choir wore floor-length sapphire blue dresses designed by the cast of *Dynasty.* They had puffy sleeves and a pointy waist and nobody looked good in them, not even after we liquored up the audience before concerts. "Big Blue," we called them, and we hoisted them on hangers to our dorm rooms before concerts, then high-heeled back across campus at twilight dressed this way, dressed like the Reagan Administration Fashion Brigade.

Once we wore them to a fundraising affair, at which an alumna was so appalled that she sat down and wrote the director a big fat dress-replacing check before the last vibrato shook itself from the ceiling. Big Blue was unceremoniously chucked in favor of stretchy black dresses, which were somewhat less hilarious but not nearly as character-building. I sorrowed quietly as I handed over Big Blue, having secretly adored myself in the satiny billows, soothed that on the outside, anyway, I was a walking symbol of the campus concept of Good Singer.

A *black* dress, of all things. You go to an SYR in a black dress. Sapphire blue is for vocal royalty.

When I was a sophomore, we performed a Latin piece in honor of the inauguration of a new College president, and it ended with a trio of shouted *"Vivat!"s,* and my desire to throw in corresponding arm-pumps practically caved the stage in, but I clenched my music folder. Now was not the time to be myself. I had to be *better* than her, up here, with everybody looking.

chapter nine

✳ ✳ ✳

Why I Couldn't Sit

Now is the part in which I tell you about how I couldn't sit down.

The campus visit I made as a high school senior that I mentioned earlier? The one with the two Domers and the Ironing Board As Table? Yeah...they offered me a chair that night, and I refused it, because my tripping neurons had convinced me chemically, if not intellectually, that if I sat in a chair a man had just vacated, I would conceive.

You try explaining this to your campus hostesses.

I stood all night.

The Jimmy Buffett music Amy burst in upon during Orientation had been hand-edited, heavily, an OCD remix with all the sex and drugs and swearing removed, which, where Buffett is concerned, left approximately four-second song clips: "Good times and riches and son-of-a (click, snap) I've seen more than I can recall." If people knew I was listening to such things, I decided as I scrubbed my hands down to the sinew in order to avoid contracting syphilis through the library book I'd just touched, well, they'd think I was weird.

"So the base of Maslow's pyramid model, one of the primary characteristics a person or society must enjoy before becoming fully self-actualized, is a feeling of safety and security," one of my high school teachers announced when I was sixteen, tapping a chalk-dust triangle that stretched from the ledge to the classroom clock. "If that's not present, the other levels—social needs, self-respect, creative outlet—will have nothing to build on."

I drew the fat first two levels in my notebook and stopped, staring: that was enough, that was too much to grapple for; when the gentle grade of "security" is itself a goal, who stood a chance with the social needs and the creative outlets? Why couldn't I just have a dysfunctional family like the other girls?

I discovered the name of why I acted the way I did, the lifelong endless ache to twirl before entering a room, at the Saint Mary's Counseling Center in the first semester of my freshman year. I went in for stress therapy and walked out with a diagnosis. A staff member took one look at my raw hands and haunted, hunted eyes and said, in effect, "Um..."

A psychiatrist wearing a Phantom of the Opera sweatshirt gave me little peach pills that made me not fear the number three so much. In about four weeks I was able to try on swimsuit bottoms in department stores again (AIDS! Microbes! Cancer! Baby out of wedlock!)

Otherwise, I just washed my hands. A lot.

What OCD does is make you do things you don't want to, and then lie about it. Kind of like alcohol, only without the pleasant warming sensation. The most infamous form of OCD is incessant cleaning and straightening rituals, but anyone within a fourteen-foot radius of 212 Regina could testify that this was not the case where I was concerned.

Instead my OCD decided to barnacle itself to my sexuality, what there was of it. Maybe my Catholicism is tied up in this; maybe not. I never hung around enough male reproductive organs to find out for sure. I would have attended Saint Mary's even if I didn't feel that I had to tap a table four times before I got up from it, but it certainly made choosing a desk infinitely easier.

Most of the time—for me, anyway—there exists no connection between satisfying the whims of the OCD and specific catastrophic events; i.e., if I don't enter the grocery through this specific door, Cincinnati Reds relief pitcher Kent Mercker will die. It's more of a vague wash of unease, a chiggering sense of "Oh Lord, I wish I hadn't done that, now what's gonna happen?"

For example.

Let's say you're walking through a public parking lot. There's a row of cars between you and the sidewalk you need to reach. There are seven spaces and six cars, parked like so:

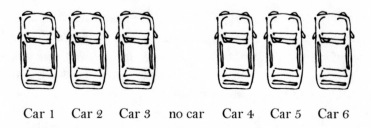

Car 1   Car 2   Car 3   no car   Car 4   Car 5   Car 6

Now: which cars do you walk past to reach the sidewalk?

The proper answer, of course, is: "The *hell?*"

But this is a scenario that could leave me psychologically rooted to the blacktop, trying to determine the path which will least piss off the OCD, which strongly dislikes the numbers three and six and is the sickest, most exacting, most finicky master in the history of ever. If neurons could talk, this is what you would hear:

ME: There's a row of cars up ahead.

OCD: Oh, better count them.

ME: Screw you. I'm not counting anything.

OCD: Count them count them count them count them!

ME: Fine, there are six, you *sick freak*, are you happy now?

OCD: Oh… dear. Six. I don't like that.

ME: It doesn't matter. Just walk.

OCD: Wait wait, you have to figure out how to walk through the cars first.

ME: All right, fine, we'll walk through Car Two and Car Three.

OCD: Oh, well—you just *go* ahead and walk past the third car. I hope you're ready to deal with the consequences.

ME: All right all right, *fine*. Between Car One and Car Two then.

OCD: You stupid git, Car One is as bad as Car Three. What if you count them from left to right? Which number is it then? Car Six. You feel like walking past a Car Six?

ME: Okay, we'll walk between Car Four and Car Five then.

OCD: I do hope you're kidding.

ME: Shut up, shut up! There's no way around this one! I have to walk past *something!* Lookit, there's a car coming—people are going to *know that this conversation is even taking place.* I'm walking through the empty space.

OCD: OH GOD, now you're between TWO cars that could possibly be Number Three Cars!

This all takes place within a manner of nanoseconds; not long enough to irretrievably ensnarl my day in an OCD-blocked traffic jam, not even long enough to perceptibly slow my steps, but pause sufficient to reflect that a grown woman with a campus job and keys to her very own dorm room was counting her college life away, car by car.

chapter ten

Otherwise Known As

I will have you know that the very first wireless message in the whole United States was sent from the then-all male University of Notre Dame to Saint Mary's College in 1899.

Run, respectively, by the Congregation of the Holy Cross and the Congregation of the Sisters of the Holy Cross, the two schools attempted a merger in the 1970's, and both loved the idea, and everybody was so busy holding press conferences and changing stationery and ripping the urinals out of the Notre Dame classroom buildings that they forgot to make sure that all parties involved wanted the same pizza toppings. Unable to bear the strain of hashing out a host of administrative details, the whole smash imploded, leaving bureaucratic shrapnel all over the Avenue.

The way I hear it, Saint Mary's understood the deal to include some sort of autonomy, and Notre Dame understood the deal to include Saint Mary's pretty much ceasing to exist. So they called it off, *mergus interruptus,* and Notre Dame simply re-understood the deal all the way to co-education.

Saint Mary's stayed put.

For thirty years, the two eyed one another from across the street.

Picture it: December, 1995. A young girl walks cold and Spanish-illiterate in the flatlands of Indiana.

I was returning from choir practice to Regina, ducking under the sleigh bells I'd hung from the door jamb. Much of the corridor was standing around in the hall.

"GOOD THING THAT WAS A TOTALLY IDIOTIC THING TO DO, AMY," Edmonds was announcing to the entirety of North tower.

"Good thing I am a *total dumbass,*" my next door neighbor announced into a copy of Plato's dialogues, which was propped open against her face. She was lying with her head on the floor, legs in her room, hair and torso in the hallway.

I dumped my books into 212. "What's going on?"

"Amy," Anne said, highlighting a passage in her early childhood development text, "just answered a call from some guy with 'Happy Thursday!'"

I pointed and laughed, for we were a supportive community, there in our women's college.

Amy continued to talk to the words pressed up against her nose. "I thought it was my *mother* calling."

Patty flung her door open. "Anyone know what the entree is tonight at the Dining Hall?"

"What did he say?" asked Justine.

"They're serving some sort of chicken on a stick," Kathy answered Patty, carrying a load of whites back from the laundry room. "I love how clean smells," she said, burying her face in the bundle.

"I didn't give him a chance to say *anything,*" said Amy. "I hung up right after he told me who he was. Good thing I am so *stupid,* you guys."

Patty sprayed cleaning fluid on the memo board stuck on her door. "Are you sure it isn't taco night?"

"Just call him *back,*" said Kathy.

"She can't call him back," said Justine. "She's destroyed herself."

"I would call him back," Kathy advised, folding underwear.

My phone rang. "Don't answer it 'Happy Thursday!'" Amy yelled, her voice still muffled by Plato.

"Something tells me it's not a guy anyway," I said, getting to my feet to retrieve the single-ringing phone. Calls from within the Saint Mary's campus sounded with one long trill; calls from outside the phone system came in with two short rings—a signal that they might have been dialed from a male-containing dorm across the street. These were generally answered with much more alacrity.

It was Carah with a homework question. I glanced down at the answering machine, which was blinking.

"Did you try to call me before?"

"No."

I hung up, hit the "play" button and started moving books from my backpack to my desk. "You have reached the secretary of Mary Beth Ellis," announced the voice of my brother-in-law, who hooked up the machine when I moved in. "Miss Ellis is in conference with Lou Holtz right now and cannot come to the phone. Please leave your name and number, and if she deigns to do so she will return your call at her earliest possible convenience. Thank you." Beep.

What I heard next was something I had never heard on my answering machine: the voice of a male other than Britton. "Um... This is the secretary of James Sotis, also known as the Notre Dame Leprechaun," came an amused voice. "He would very much like to speak with Miss Ellis, so if you could please tell her to return a call to him he would very much appreciate it. Thank you and have a good evening."

¡Dímelo tú! crashed to the floor.

It had been over a month since—Why was he—

My door flew open and Amy, just missing the bells, came barreling through it. "MB!" she screeched, shoving me against the desk. "M*B!*"

"Ow!"

"But *Mary Beth!*" She pushed again, and I ricocheted into my desk chair. *"The Leprechaun called you!"*

"I thought you wanted to be dead."

She grabbed my answering machine. "Can I borrow this for a sec?"

"Amy, wait—"

She ran to the door and screamed down the hall. "Justine! Kathy! Patty! Grace!" She turned her head and screamed in the other direction. "Anne! Edmonds! Carah!"

"Carah lives *three stories away.*"

"Good thing I *can't believe* this." She bounced back to my machine as Justine came in, short enough that she didn't set off the bells.

"Most of them went to the Hall Council meeting," she said. "What?"

Amy played the message. Justine stared. "What exactly is it that you do," she said, "when the rest of us go out and have lives?"

"You guys, seriously—"

The sleigh bells signaled Anne's entrance, even though the room capacity had been exceeded two people ago. "You wanna help me study history?" she said.

"Good thing you're about to be shocked out of your mind," said Amy. "Mary Beth is *BF's* with the Leprechaun."

"I am not best friends with the Leprechaun."

Anne gaped at me. "No way!"

Amy played the message.

Anne continued to gape at me. "No way!"

"When's he calling again?" said Justine.

I dry heaved a little and leaned my head against a sign a family member had made for me: "THE BELLE OF SAINT MARY'S LIVES HERE."

Anne ran out the door. "I have to tell Carah!" she said over the jingling.

Amy played the message again.

"That is so cool," said Justine.

Right here. Right here on my little square of a Wal-Mart carpet, I was going to be sick.

An out-of-breath Anne returned. "Carah's not home," she said. "I left a note. You're calling him back, right, MB?"

"Are you people, like, my personal beeper service?"

"She can do it from Anne's room," decided Justine. "There's an extension in there. We can all listen."

"She can't *call* him," said Amy. "You can't *call* a guy. Or answer when he does."

"But he told her to call," said Justine. "Let's go, MB. Do you have the Leprechaun's number?"

"He has a *name*," I said.

"Look him up in the student directory. What dorm does the Leprechaun live in?"

"I can't call him! I don't know what to *say*." I opened my theology notebook to a fresh page. "Lemmie write a script."

I thought Amy was going to die. *"Script?"*

"I don't know what I'm doing!"

Justine picked up a pair of underwear Kathy had dropped on her way back from the laundry room and twirled it around a finger as I worked. Anne looked over my shoulder. "What do you have written down so far?" she said.

"I have 'Hi.'"

"I wonder what he wants," Anne said.

"I bet I know," said Amy. "I bet he saw her from afar and fell *madly in love* with her but didn't have the nerve to call her earlier and now he wants to, like, take her out and propose at *Le Mans Tower* or something so they can have little SMC-Leprechaun babies."

"I bet that's it," Justine agreed.

"Or," I said, "he could be a nice guy and decided to call me and thank me for writing the stupid let—" I stopped, closing my eyes.

"Oh. My. GOD," said Amy.

"Fan mail?" said Justine. "You wrote fan mail to the Leprechaun?"

"I wouldn't call it *fan*—"

"You are *sick!*"

"Okay. Waitwaitwaitwait. You know the profile they did on him in *The Observer* before the last home game?"

They did not.

"So they did this article on him, and he seemed really nice, and does a lot of volunteer work, and he mentioned Saint Mary's and that he likes that we go to the games too, and I thought that was cool of him, right, and I thought it would be nice if I thanked him for mentioning us, so... I kind of..."

"Wrote him a *fan letter.*" Amy snatched the notebook away and beat me with it. "Lame, lame, *lame!* OH my God! *Eng*lish majors! You *never* tell a guy that you think he seems really nice. Or 'thank you.' *Ever!*"

"Or else what?"

"Or else he'll never *ca*—"

The room went silent for a moment.

Amy returned the notebook. "Finish the stupid script."

Half an hour later we were assembled in Anne's room. "Okay," our hostess said, flipping through her student directory. "Sotis." She read off his number.

I was gripping one receiver; Amy, Justine, and Anne were crowded around the other. "Hold it," I said. "I can hear you guys breathing."

Justine covered the speaking end of their receiver with her hand. I listened again.

"Now I can hear you guys breathing *and* Justine's hand on the phone."

"You can't hear a *hand,*" she objected. I gave her the receiver. She put it to her ear, still holding onto the other phone. "Well," she said, and held out my receiver to Amy. "Does this sound like a hand to you?"

I wiped my palms on the wall.

Anne reached into her dresser and pulled out a pair of socks. "Here," she said, unrolling them. "Try this."

Amy pulled a sock over the receiver. "Safe phone sex," she said.

"How's it sound now?" Anne asked.

I listened. "Much better."

"Good thing it's *all you* now, MB," Amy said.

I reached for the dialing pad, then stopped. "I forgot his number."

Justine exhaled very loudly. "He'll be graduated by the time you get around to it," she said, grabbing the directory and dialing the number for me.

One ring. Two rings. Three rings. Four. Voice mail.

I slammed down the receiver; they yelped. "Well, now I need a whole *new* script," I said.

"You do *not*." Justine hit the redial button on the Sock Phone. "You will leave a message, and you will leave one *now*."

"But I—" The voice mail beeped. "Hi, Jamey?" I rushed out. "This is Mary Beth. Sorry I missed you. We're playing phone tag, and you're it. Bye." I hung up and dropped my head between my knees.

"Awesome ," said Amy, pronouncing it "oh-uh-sume".

"It was *not*," I said. "'You're *it*'? That's worse than 'Happy Thursday.'"

"Nothing's worse than 'Happy Thursday.'" said Anne.

"I thought it was cute," Justine said.

"Now what?" I said.

"Now," said Amy, "you *wait*. But when you answer the phone, you make it seem like you *haven't* been waiting."

We looked at the clock. 8:09.

"I'm tired of waiting," said Anne.

"Yeah," said Amy. "Let's watch *Friends*. You're the only one on this side of the hall that gets reception, MB. We have to be in your room anyway."

"I have to study," said Justine. "I'll be in my room." She left, snorting something about hands and socks.

We returned to 212. I jittered back and forth along the two feet of floor between my sink and the door.

"MB," Anne said, "you're making me seasick over here."

"Sorry," I said, and started pacing off the distance between the sink and the TV set instead.

"All right," Anne said, turning off a whiny Monica. "Time for some mental health activity."

"That's what I was doing."

"That was wearing a hole in the floor. We need to do something constructive." She reached for my bottom desk drawer. "You still got those bead ornament kits you brought back from Thanksgiving?"

"Yes. We can make either bells or candy canes."

"Dibs on a bell," Amy said. Amy was also the type of person to yell "Shotgun!" and "Firsties!" and "Go to hell, *I'm* licking bowl."

I said, "Let's go in the hall. The walls are closing in."

"Could be the two inch-thick layer of *crap* you've got on them," Amy muttered, following me into the corridor, but not before meeting my Christmas decorations headfirst. "GOOD THING I AM SICK OF LIVING NEXT TO A LIQUOR STORE, MB," she screamed, swatting the sleigh bells aside.

I slid down the wall to the floor.

"Now," Anne said placidly, breaking the cellophane with her teeth and dumping beads on the floor. "Suppose you tell me why you're acting like you've suddenly developed some sort of bodily attention deficit disorder."

Amy handed me the directions. I tossed them away. "Other than the fact that the same guy who does the touchdown push ups in front of the whole entire world just called her?" she said. *"Her? A SMC? A freshman SMC?* Somebody who—"

I started jamming red and white pinwheel beads onto a pipe cleaner, then dropped it to place my hands on the opposite side of the corridor. I kicked my feet out behind me. Arms and legs tight.

"You know, MB," Amy said, watching me work my way to the ceiling, "I've known you for about six months now, and honestly? I don't think that's good for your skin tone."

I dropped back to the floor and picked up my pipe cleaner again. "I didn't go to my senior prom, okay?"

They sat. I added another bead.

"Or my junior one."

They continued to sit.

"Or the Sophomore Formal." I crammed on a white pinwheel. "Or—"

Anne frowned. "But I saw a picture of you in your senior year-book wearing—"

"I worked the concession stand," I said, with the pipe cleaner full of beads and little idea what to do next. "The Senior Class Council assumed I wouldn't be going, and they asked me to work the concession stand."

"Oh," said Anne.

"*Weak*," said Amy.

"It doesn't matter," I told them.

Amy looked at me. "I think it does."

Anne held up a tiny, tacky bead bell.

"How'd you do that?" I said.

"It's called following the directions. Look. You bend the wire like this—"

My phone double-rang.

Amy grabbed my arm. "At *least* three rings," she said.

I shook her off, ducking into the doorway. "When the Leprechaun starts calling *you*, you can not-answer the phone any way you want."

I faced the phone, horrible thing. Could I get pregnant if I even—"Hello?"

"Is Mary Beth there?"

"This is she."

"You're it."

✳ ✳ ✳

Ten minutes later I gathered Amy, Anne, and Justine in my room. "Okay," I said, clenching my hands together. "Okay."

Anne was jumping up and down. "So?"

"Jamey's gonna be here in fifteen minutes to pick me up."

They screamed at volumes usually reserved for hailing one another across the quad. "What did he *say?*" said Amy. "Tell me *exactly* what he said."

"He said, 'I'll be there in fifteen minutes to pick you up.'"

"Wow," Anne breathed.

"What's he like, what's he like?" said Amy.

"Oh! So nice. He's funny, he's kind—"

Justine leaned against the wall. "He's magically delicious."

"Fifteen *minutes?*" said Amy, running to my closet and flinging it open. "Did he say what you guys are going to do?"

"He runs a Bible study group at Notre Dame, and they're all getting together to watch a movie tonight. He asked me if I wanted to go."

Amy whirled around, holding one of my skirts. "MB, do you know what this *is?*"

"A cotton-poly blend?"

"Not *this.*" She threw the skirt back in the closet and pointed to my phone. "*That.* You are about to go on a *date*, Mary Beth."

"And you don't even have to take the *bus*," Justine said admiringly.

My pregnancy-fearing OCD burst to the surface, Shamu rising from ordinarily still waters. "It is *not!*"

"It is! It involves *your* phone and *his* car. It's a date."

"What's a date? Who has one?" said Kathy, jingling into 212. Well, good. The Regina Hall Council meeting was now reconvening in my room.

"Mary Beth does," said Anne. "With the Leprechaun."

Kathy laughed.

"It's NOT A DATE. And don't tell anybody, okay?"

"Katie! Guess what!" Kathy yelled as Edmonds walked by on the way to her room.

"Wait—" I said. Not Edmonds. Not CBS, the Campus Broadcasting System.

Too late. "MARY BETH HAS A DATE WITH THE LEPRECHAUN??!!" Edmonds thundered. In a jingling roar, the remaining members of Two North stampeded into 212.

Amy hit the play button on my answering machine.

In his car! I was going to have to be with a boy and sit in his car; maybe he'd had sex in that car, and there was, you know, *stuff* left over—

"Girls!" The RA peeked her head in. "It's getting a little loud in here."

"Laura!" Amy screeched. "Mary Beth is going on a date with the Leprechaun!"

"That's nice," said Laura, and left.

"When did he ask you?" Patty wanted to know.

"About eight twenty," I said.

"I can't believe it!"

"I know," I said, looking around for a place to vomit discreetly.

Patty was incredulous. "No, I mean—he called you during *Friends?* You didn't miss anything, did you?"

Amy shoved her way into her room and returned with an armload of eyeshadow.

"You can't go on a date without some makeup," she said. "Good thing you look like death on a hot plate."

"THIS IS NOT A DATE!" I needed air. I pushed past my corridormates into the hall, colliding into my sleigh bells with greater force than usual. "Ow!"

"Can he bring some friends?" said Grace. She was cleaning her ROTC rifle.

"When's he getting here?" Kathy asked.

I laid down on the carpet and concentrated on inhaling at regular intervals. "Not soon enough."

Patty's boyfriend was visiting from across the street. "Isn't he a little old for you?" he said.

I threw a green bead at him.

"I want to meet Jamey," said Anne.

"YEAH!" Edmonds took off running back to her room, hurdling over me in the hall. Beads scattered everywhere.

"Here! Wear this!" came Amy's voice as a pair of khakis and cranberry turtleneck landed on my head.

I shoved them aside. "I refuse to change my clothes."

A vent brush came flying after them. "At least do something with your hair."

"Yes. Okay. See if Kathy will let me borrow her Cher wig."

Anne said, "Bring him up here!"

"I am not bringing him anywhere near this hallway."

"Why not?"

Edmonds came running back down the hall with a camera. "IS HE HERE YET?"

"There will *be no* photographic equipment," I screamed, sitting up.

"But it's not every day you decide to get a social life with a campus celebrity," said Patty.

Enough. I stood to address the throng of corridormates packed into my room. "Look," I said, "I told Jamey to call up from the lobby when he gets here. If you want to go on Leprechaun Watch, I suggest you do it from there."

They took off running.

"And don't be obvious!"

They returned, grabbed notebooks and texts, and took off running again.

I buried my face in my hands.

Carah, newly arrived from the fifth floor, stayed behind. "I know you're scared," she said, hugging me. "I'll stay here and go down with you."

"Thank you." She was the only one who knew about the amber vials in my medicine cabinet.

"I'm so happy for you, MB."

"Carah—"

She smoothed my hair. "Hmmm?"

"You know that if you walk down with me I have to introduce you to Jamey, don't you."

She smiled at me. "I'm so happy for you, MB."

The phone rang. Single ring this time. Jamey Sotis had entered the building. I sucked in air a couple times, then picked up. So this is what happens when you expand your social network to people with Y chromosomes: An ulcer by the age of nineteen.

"Hello?"

"MB?"

"Amy?"

"MB, good thing your date's here. We just saw his car pull in the lot."

"Good thing he's *not my date*. Where are you calling from?"

"The *lobby*, moron."

"Are you out of your mind?"

I heard Edmonds in the background. "WHAT KIND OF CAR DOES HE HAVE?"

"Ohmigod! He's coming down the walk—no, wait, I think he forgot something, he's going back to his car..."

"Amy, I really don't need a play by play analysis."

"Okay, he's coming back again. He's *cute* close up, Mary Beth. All those push-ups really—"

"He's coming *in!*" hissed Patty. "Hang *up!*"

"Wait, I want to tell her how he—" The line went dead.

I replaced the receiver and banged my head against the loft.

"Stop that!" said Carah. "You'll mess up your bangs."

The phone rang again with the actual Jamey, and Carah and I started for the lobby. Down the stairs, out the detexed staircase door, through the lounge.

I stopped Carah just before we entered the lobby. "He really is just being a nice guy, isn't he?" I said in low tones.

"I think that's a safe assumption to make." She squeezed my fingers. "Your hands are *freezing*."

"Why is this happening?"

"Because after eighteen years," she said giving me a gentle push towards the lobby, "it's time to come out from behind the concession stand."

He was sitting in the puke orange vinyl chair manufactured during the Johnson Administration that every guy sat in when he came calling at Regina.

"Jamey?" I said.

It was a stupid question. He was wearing a Notre Dame cheerleading jacket with an ND cheerleading baseball cap. Also, the beard.

"Hi there, Mary Beth," he said hugging me. I angled away from him so that we were in contact only from the waist up. Over his shoulder I could see Two North pretending, very badly, to be engrossed in study materials. Edmonds was holding *¡Dímelo tú!* upside down.

I glared. They waved.

"You ready?" he said after I presented an awed Carah. I nodded, prepared to barrel ingloriously through Regina's doors as I did every day on my way to class. He beat me to it, holding the door open for me. "Thanks," I said, more out of shock than politeness.

One of my blue SMC gloves fluttered to the pavement on our way to the parking lot. I stopped short, turned around, and was about to bend over when I saw the entirety of Two North crowded around the door of Regina, faces mashed against the glass. Amy was wiping away tears.

Jamey had stopped too. "Do you know them?" he asked.

I retrieved the runaway glove. "They're just some people who are too annoying to live with and too amusing to kill."

He looked at them, then back at me. "The housing computer can throw you together with total freaks freshman year," he said.

"If you're lucky," I told him, throwing the huddled mass at the door a small high sign as I pretended to put the glove on. They waved again, furiously.

chapter eleven

Columns

I feel I must tell you that Saint Mary's wasn't my first-choice college. That distinction belongs to the United States Air Force Academy. I wanted to be an astronaut, and astronauts seemed to issue from the Air Force Academy on a regular basis, plus it was located in Colorado Springs, and Colorado Springs meant horses would probably be hanging around somewhere nearby. Yes, I would ride horses! During my down time! In space!

Then I turned thirteen and high school algebra came upon me, and that, of course, was that for the Air Force Academy. "Astronauts kind of need to be able to add and subtract without counting on their fingers," the guidance counselor said gently.

Well—what else was there?

Writing glided easily from me, which caught my attention because absolutely nothing else did except occasional bouts of furor. I didn't show early scholastic skill in the English language, largely because my primary linguistics education consisted of filling out many perforated workbook pages, and, as I had the fine motor skills of an aircraft carrier, my workbook pages always looked as though they'd been pre-chewed by a wolverine, so I would get marked down. But I filled notebooks with poorly printed crap for fun, without classroom prompting, and I told stories to my big sister to lull her to sleep. My mother, a teacher, handed me pencils and Newbery Medal books and held her breath.

When I was fourteen, just as the Academy Chapel slid out of my scholastic rearview mirror, I accompanied my parents to find a car for my sister to drive us to school. It was a horrible and long and boring experience, and I wrote about it and sent it to a magazine and they printed it even though the title was—are you ready? Are you ready? You have to be ready for this, for how great this is—"When Buying Your Dream Car Becomes a Nightmare." I got zero money but a free copy of the magazine and a congratulatory letter with my name spelled wrong, which turned out to be the most realistic literary training I would ever receive.

So. Writing, then. Perhaps NASA would have need of a professional evaluator of Jane Austen on a future space shuttle mission. I learned to touch-type and ran my high school's literary magazine, which basically consisted of wrangling nine hundred pages of depressing poetry. Also I drank tea and was very very weird, which, I felt, were pretty much the sole requirements for writerdom.

I also wrote for my high school paper, *The Etcetera*, because when you're looking for a no-nonsense, smashmouth journalism name, what you want is something that says "I would provide further evidence, but don't particularly feel like it." Produced by the journalism class, *The Etcetera* had a circulation of eighteen homerooms. When laying out the pages for the printer, we stood at tilted tables and cut our typed stories into columns, then taped them to poster board superimposed with pale blue graph lines. I was a senior before I realized that *The Washington Times* was not put together with masking tape and Wite-Out.

Various, actual headlines from my *Etcetera* era:

"CINCINNATI REDS' RANKS REEK"
"GLOBAL EVENTS TRANSPIRED THIS YEAR"
"DYNAMIC DUOS DARE TO DANCE"

We used a *lot* of Wite-Out.

I wrote humor columns for *The Etcetera* and decided to stick with that as a career, because they seemed less bother than a novel. My classmates at the college prep high school I attended, they wanted to be environmental engineers and physical therapists and corporate lawyers. My contribution to the world would be: More "When Buying Your Dream Car Becomes a Nightmare."

The way to go about this, I was told, was to become a journalist, pay my dues for eight or nine hundred years covering garden parties and dog fashion shows, and then, maybe, if I was a good girl, I might be eligible for a column just as I was ready for retirement. The prospect of this made me frowny, but all other career options involved math, other people, and children, so I began searching out strong writing colleges.

"Small, liberal arts school," everybody said, and I thought briefly about Bowling Green State University, and its excellent journalism program, but I took one look at its largely metal campus and its *orange and brown* school colors and ran screaming back to square one. Priorities.

Saint Mary's, however, sirened me in with the English writing major and the senior thesis project, in which we were required to, in essence, write a book. Boom! I would emerge from the college womb Random House-ready and agent prepped!

There was also *The Observer,* the student newspaper shared with Notre Dame. There was no faculty advisor and it was produced on a daily basis, highly unusual for a campus paper; most tend to trickle onto the quads when the staff's beer money runs out and some econ major remembers to turn in the five thousand word feature on the two frat guys who decorated their entire apartment with bottle caps. *The Observer,* though—these people were *serious.* They had stationery. And a *water cooler.*

The first issue I ever saw of *The Observer* came out on the first day of my campus visit. I spread it on the carpet square resting on the concrete floor of my hostess' dorm room, staring at the head-shots of the upperclassmen with the editorial columns. I pointed.

"Can *anyone* do that?" I said.

They exchanged glances. "Not if you want to have a social life," one said.

Done and done.

The Observer offices, during my tenure, were located in Notre Dame's LaFortune Student Center. I could not get enough of LaFortune, which had a florist's shop and a video store offering up to ten VHS tapes in stock at once in the basement. Post-midnight, the snack bar (named—this is the best—"The Huddle") began selling quarter dogs, which were greenish hot dogs for a quarter apiece. You always got your money's worth, with a quarter dog. They were the sole energy force of the entire editorial staff.

Just as I began writing for *The Observer*, political satirist P.J. O'Rourke came to campus. I bought tickets. *He* was a humor columnist. Maybe he could give me the name of his editor, because clearly, what with all the masking tape, I was qualified for at least a biweekly syndicated slot somewhere.

O'Rourke appeared at Stepan Center, which was largely notable for possessing the worst acoustics this side of screaming into a toilet bowl. On the outside, Stepan looked exactly like the exterior of a halved Wiffle Ball, but things vastly improved once you got to the inside, which looked exactly like the interior of a halved Wiffle Ball settled over an enormous cookie sheet. And when our guest took the podium, he shuffled his notes briefly and said, "Thank you for inviting me to your fine school, and this very attractive building."

There was a reception for O'Rourke hosted by the Student Council afterwards, and I hung back from the crowd, watching wave after wave of Belles and Domers press adoringly up against him, offering to buy drinks. This, then, cemented my career choice: If you become a successful writer, people will give you beer. Screw you, Air Force Academy and becoming an astronaut! You can't fit a keg into an F-16!

I made my way to the big famous author's side and asked him for some Advice To A Young Writer, and he thought for a moment and said, "Go to dental school."

The Observer was not, for some reason, impressed with GLOBAL EVENTS TRANSPIRED THIS YEAR and sent me to cover such hard-hitting campus issues as a revamping of Saint Mary's literary magazine, *Chimes*, a name which left an impression at least as commanding as *The Etcetera* ("For whom do these *Chimes* tinkle?")

I wrote: "Literary semi-chaos ensued."

And: "The editors are not alone in their quest to make *Chimes* ring brighter than ever this year."

And: "Whether a Saint Mary's student submits a poem, play, or essay, she contributes to this worthy outlet for her creative energy."

Then the features section assigned me to compare Notre Dame's library to Saint Mary's.

I wrote: "The neon green of the Saint Mary's elevator alarms the casual visitor."

And: "Whether they prefer to face the core task of college huddled in a carrel squirreled away from the world or propped up at a table amidst the hum of steady conversation, the students of this community are sure to find a place to feel at home."

A month later, somebody called my dorm room in search of a profile of a Saint Mary's student in the process of integrating with a mostly-Notre Dame organization. So I hung up, and, with my vast Serious Investigative Reporter Skills firmly in place, walked two doors down to Justine's room. She had just joined the Notre Dame Chorale, a classical vocal group.

I wrote: "With two brothers as Domer alums, this sophomore's ties to the Notre Dame family run deep and fascinating."

And: "Whether she's singing in a Saint Mary's shower or sharing her gift with her Notre Dame brothers and sisters, she invites us to enjoy her considerable vocal talent."

A fellow Regina resident named Rosalinda alerted me in the second semester that a position was open at *The Observer* for a Saint Mary's features editor, and suggested that I apply. I perked up immediately, for here was an opportunity to use "whether" on a power basis.

"Why is there an opening?" I said. "Did somebody graduate?"

"Nah," she said. "The one we have now is studying in Australia for a year."

The fact that people were leaving the hemisphere to escape *The Observer* did not occur to me at the time, so I applied, and when I showed up for the interview, the senior Saint Mary's editor, Sarah, and the Notre Dame features editor, Lynn, were waiting for me with folded arms. Lynn was wearing a T-shirt that read "Feed Kate Moss."

Sarah held up my resume. "It says here that you worked on your high school newspaper," she said. "Our primary software programs are Quark Express and WordPerfect 5.1. What system did your high school use?"

"Masking tape," I said.

"Is that anything like Windows?" asked Lynn.

"Probably."

"You'll catch on," she said. "Here's the deal. Your official title will be Saint Mary's features editor and Notre Dame assistant features editor. That means you'll be responsible for all the cultural activities going on at SMC as well as a two-page features spread one day a week."

I nodded.

Sarah said, "We'll have a Saint Mary's staff meeting each Sunday night where we'll discuss what's going on at your campus that could go into your section. After that we'll have a features staff meeting when you'll run your ideas for the section by Lynn here. Then you'll assign the stories, check to make sure they're in a few days before you put the section together, and get in touch with the staff members who do the photos and the art. Then you check the art, copy edit it, lay it out, and wait for the managing editor on duty to approve everything. Got it?"

"Um."

"By the way," said Lynn, punching the down button on the LaFortune elevator, "you're hired."

I called ahead to Two North with the news, and when I got back to Regina 212 I found a sign hanging on my door: "Say Hi to the New Saint Mary's Features Editor!" Its letters had been cut from magazine ads, ransom-note style.

"Thanks, guys!" I hollered.

"You're welllllllcome!" peppered from various doorways.

"DON'T SUCK, OKAY?" issued from Edmonds'.

I went to bed and was awakened by a scraping noise outside my door. I checked the clock. 2:14 AM.

It's just the wind.

Scrape.

It's just the wind, breaking and entering.

Scrape.

I scrambled from my loft and slammed around in the dark, searching for a weapon. At last my fingers closed around a squishy, fuzz-covered object. I turned it over. Hemingway.

Okay. Homicide by stuffed pelican.

Scrape.

Clutching Hemingway by the beak, I crept towards the door, preparing to fling it open with a women's college warrior screech. I pulled the fling off beautifully and was primed to execute the yell when I saw Rosalinda on her hands and knees, in the act of shoving something under my door.

I socked her one with Hemingway. "You're lucky I couldn't find my curling iron."

She got up. "Sorry. I didn't mean to wake you. I just came in from the office and wanted to give you this." She held out a fresh pad of *Observer* notepaper.

I hugged her, squinting from the lights coming from Kathy's room down the hall; she was barely getting started on the evening's homework. "Oh, thank you. That's awfully sweet."

"No problem. Welcome to the Big O," she said, picking up her backpack.

"Rosa!" I called, stepping onto the hall carpet so my bare feet wouldn't freeze to the linoleum in my room. "Did you say you just got *in?*"

She nodded. "I had to copy edit tonight."

"What kind of—"

I heard a shoe strike the inside of the door of 211. "Good thing I can *never get any sleep* around here," Amy yelled. "SHUT UP!"

I dropped my voice in order to avoid unleashing hell to pay, Jersey style, and said, "Is this usually when you get in?"

She shrugged. "Nah. We finished early tonight."

I gazed at her.

"Well," said my new colleague, cheerfully slinging her backpack over her shoulder, "time to get some homework done. See you at the staff meeting Sunday!"

I went back to bed, dreading further global events transpiring.

✳ ✳ ✳

Lynn ran alongside me for my first week of editoring, then ripped away the training wheels. The bike immediately went over a cliff.

My first solo spread addressed vegetarianism at Saint Mary's. I assigned reporters to see who hung around the tofu at the dining hall salad bar and mashed together a collection of non-meat recipes. I decided to have the artist who was working that night frame the articles and sidebars with drawings of vines. The news-hungry public, I very firmly felt, was clamoring for a good vine.

The Observer had recently shifted to an all-computer format, but what was not explained to me during my probing job interview was that the computers were run by sixth-grade science fair electricity experiments. I dropped my backpack next to the features desk and logged in. I was greeted by a wait message. Then: gears shifting beneath the monitor.

Okay. Okay. I poised my hands over the keyboard.

The monitor screen flickered, and presented... another wait message.

When I was at last able to open the lead article, the copy was about a hundred and fifty words short of what I'd asked for. A responsible editor, in this situation, calls in the author, places a hand on his or her shoulder, and patiently guides the journalist in producing the required copy, explaining along the way that truly great news writing is a product of tight word choice and vivid exploration.

I found a thesaurus and triple-spaced the paragraphs.

There.

I went back to the production office for layout.

Production involved huge, complicated, expensive computers that arranged the text, placed headlines, and imported photos and art. They were the antithesis of the computers in the main *Observer* office in the sense that they were supposed to make our jobs faster instead of turning it into one big scene from *Waiting for Godot*. The tradeoff, however, was that the computers in the production office were approximately as simple to master as the controls of the Hubble space telescope. Lynn and Jackie, production tech extraordinaire, gave me a crash course at the keyboard one day, and it sounded like a Pentagon briefing ("You type in the department password and give it *this* command to open a new document, and you use *this* keystroke after pulling down *that* menu to set the font point size, and if you want to drop a nuclear bomb on Iran you click on *this* icon here...")

So I was content to stick to the high-tech task of pointing to the monitor and saying "Make this headline look, you know, *newsy*" and otherwise leaving Jackie to deal with the campus NORAD, but that night a total stranger was sitting in the production office when I walked in. "Hi!" she said brightly.

I sipped at the cafe mocha I was holding. "Hi. I'm looking for the features production tech."

She smiled. "That's me!"

I sat down in front of the computer, setting my cup away from the keyboard. "But you're not Jackie."

"She's lead tech on Thursdays now. You'll be working with me for the rest of the semester. I'm Elise."

"Oh. Nice to meet you, then."

"Thanks!"

We sat there.

"Well!" I said. "Guess we better get started!"

"Guess so!" she said.

We sat there.

"Um," I hedged, "don't you think you should start placing text or something?"

"Yeah, that's probably a good idea."

We sat there.

"Well—"

"Oh," she said, "I'm a new hire. I've never actually done this before. I was kind of hoping you would know how to start."

The shuttle bus running between the campii had stopped running by the time I got out of LaFortune that night, and I had to call SMC Security for an escort back to Regina.

But Saint Mary's had never seen, in its entire 152 years, such lovingly rendered newspaper vines.

The whole affair wreaked havoc with my rapidly relaxing OCD, upending the wonders the drugs had done, forcing me to pace for hours in front of half-finished layouts. But I couldn't have just three stories; then what would happen? This line with six words—well, that would *never* do. Had I checked this student's last name was spelled correctly? And checked it? And checked it? Checked it once more so that I hadn't checked it three times?

To relieve the suicidal stress of placing my deadline in the hands of sometimes unreliable student writers and photographers, I more often than not took matters into my own word processor and wrote the bulk of the section articles myself, once even taking Carah and a cardboard camera with me to shoot the pictures I needed for a spread about campus landmarks. The shots of the Touchdown Jesus mural on the side of Notre Dame's library came out a little crooked.

"He looks like he's been out drinking," said one of the techs when I asked him to help me import the image.

"Can you blame him?"

On the nights Rosalinda and I worked together we would go down to the Huddle after the spreads were done, and engage in the important editorial task of ingesting quarter dogs and Soft Batch cookies and exchanging heartfelt agreement that nobody at all appreciated us.

Adding the burden of writing much of my week's section to the time-eating job of editing it was dragging me by the ponytail into a vortex of exhaustion.

"Mary Beth," said Lynn at one point, "you have got to slow down. I've seen this before. You are burning yourself out. Go back to Saint Mary's and get some sleep."

"Okay. Are you using that phone?" I said.

On those rare occasions when I did leave LaFortune's third floor, Two North acted as though I were a returning Odysseus, hauling a dead cyclops behind me.

"Look," said Grace when she saw me returning from class one afternoon. "I *told* you guys she didn't spontaneously combust."

"You want some orange juice?" Amy offered. "Patty just made off with a whole mugfull from the Dining Hall. The worker checking the ID's at the door yelled. It was the *best.*"

"Orange juice," I said, unlocking the door of 212 and dumping my books. "That is precisely what I need. More acid in my stomach."

She followed me. "I need to borrow your ruler."

"For what?"

"Art class. Get this. Good thing they're making us draw a *naked woman.*"

I started rooting around in my desk drawers. "Seriously?"

She nodded.

"So there is an actual model—"

"Yes. And she stands there posing with this, like, big *stick.*"

"*Completely* naked?"

"Yes! And she's *old!* Like *forty* or something. It's disgusting."

"What do you need this for?" I asked, surfacing at last with my ruler.

"To draw the stick."

I tossed a blank computer disk into my backpack, grateful that I had decided to collect my fine arts credit in a music appreciation course. "I don't want to know any more."

"Where are you going?" Amy said as I shooed her out of the room and locked the door behind me.

"Guess."

She sighed. "Good thing we all miss you. Good thing you're never *here*. Especially when I need to borrow stuff."

"I miss you guys too. But things'll slow down. I just have to get this one spread out of the way."

She inhaled deeply. "Wow. I must have missed a crapping bull when he came through here, because—"

I headed for the shuttle stop. "Tell the girls I said hi and bye."

By midterms my GPA had slid from a 3.5 to a 3.0. Spanish and bio were becoming mass critical. But every day I was presented with the following choice:

1. I could prepare for a major aspect of my future career with witty, intelligent people, once every week creating the center spread for the daily student voice of one of the foremost women's colleges in the nation, dutifully churning my two pages like a good SMC so as to avoid bringing the wrath of Lynn upon my head.

Or:

2. I could memorize another two pages of vocabulary words in *¡Dímelo tú!*

There were several nights when I dragged myself out of the office long after the last shuttle ran with burning eyes and furious back muscles. And I assistant-edited one of *The Observer's* kinder, gentler sections.

Once I came into the office to find Rosalinda on the phone in tears, interviewing the mother of a Saint Mary's junior who had succumbed to an illness she'd fought for months.

"Sometimes," she said, hanging up, "I run into news I just don't want to report."

I smoothed her hair and brought her a full cup from the water cooler. And sometimes there's nothing you can do.

✳ ✳ ✳

The next week I went to the library in an attempt to administer mouth-to-mouth resuscitation to my GPA, which was going beautifully until a hand shook my shoulder.

"Hey, girl," said a familiar voice in library tones, "wake up."

You know how sometimes you wake up in the middle of a library and the Notre Dame Leprechaun is smirking at you?

I stirred and patted the seat next to me, but not *too* next to me. "What are you doing on my side of the street?"

Jamey slid into the couch. "I think the question is, what are *you* doing on your side of the street?"

"Yeah, sorry I missed your last phone call. I'm not in my room very much these days."

He continued to smirk at me.

"What."

"Nice fashion statement," he said, indicating the two feet of toilet paper streaming from my left sneaker.

"Oh. That." I kicked the leg in the air. "It's a thing for *The Observer.* One of the editors is a psych major, and she wants to do this story on social behavior. We're supposed to purposely place ourselves in uncomfortable social situations to see if anyone says anything. You're the first. May I quote you?"

"You seem... a little... stressed."

"Of course I'm a little stressed. I'm walking around campus looking like Mr. Whipple's whore."

"No, I mean—it sounds like they kind of ask a lot of you over there."

I rubbed a hand across sandpaper eyes. "It's not that I don't appreciate the opportunity."

"But?"

"I love seeing people read my writing."

"But?"

"But this job makes me want to remove my own intestines with a *pizza cutter*," I scream-whispered.

He patted my shoulder and stood. "Listen, I need to look up some books. Can you lend me a pen?"

I handed him my Bic. He held up the chewed-on cap, which looked like the losing end of a battle between a pissy lion and a fasting puma, and looked at me. "Maybe you should slow down with this newspaper stuff."

"No way. This is my first taste of real journalism—"

"And," he said, "you're gagging on it."

✶ ✶ ✶

Lynn, preparing for graduation, was phasing herself out and phasing the new features editor in. The new editor wanted a weekly edition of the "photo poll", a random sampling of students' opinions on an issue appearing next to a small head shot of the opinionee. They were awful to find a photographer for, terrible to lay out, and horrendous to check for name-face accuracy.

Photo polls would be appearing in the features section on Wednesdays.

Wednesday was the day I was in charge of the features section.

Within two weeks, I had been threatened with a libel suit for allegedly misquoting a graduate student on the quality of the trays in North Dining Hall, fired a photographer for asking his female subjects to remove their tops "to check lighting levels," and run through *The Observer* office at a dead sprint, desk scissors pointed at my throat, yelling for people to trip me.

In the first week of March, because I truly knew how to party, I decided to complete a layout on the campus' classical music organizations. The Saint Mary's Women's Choir. The South Bend Chamber Singers.

And? The all-male University of Notre Dame Glee Club.

I assigned away the Women's Choir article and found someone to do a piece on the South Bend Symphony Orchestra.

I would write the Glee Club article.

Carah watched me at my desk, preparing a mock layout on graph paper and leaving a sizable portion of it to the Clubbers. "This," she said, "is a blatant abuse of your power as a journalist and editor."

I looked at her with wide eyes. "Why, whatever do you mean?"

"I *mean* the fact that you drooled all over your program at their last concert just might have something to do with this sudden interest in the local culture." She picked up the black-and-white publicity glossy of the tuxedo-wearing Club, shot against the serene backdrop of the Grotto.

"I want one," she said, examining the tenor section.

"Don't bend it," I said, allotting the Club article a few more column inches. Sorry, South Bend Chamber Singers.

Carah saw me do it. *"See?"*

I brushed away the eraser crumbs. "Miss Carah, you unfairly malign my journalistic intentions. The Club is marking the eightieth anniversary of its founding this year, and their Spring Concert is coming up, and they had some poor publicity last year, and I just think it's a nice human-interest article on a healthy musical outlet for the young men of this community."

She laughed very hard.

"It's not my fault I have to sit in on one of their rehearsals."

"Research, right?"

"Somebody has to do it."

Amy entered, then turned and banged on the door. "I brought your ruler back," she announced.

"Yeah… just… keep it, Amy."

"Thanks," she said cheerfully. "I'd just borrow it again anyway."

"I thought you guys were done with the nude."

"We are. Now we have to draw a bowl of fruit. I'm afraid the prof might work the stick into *that* picture, too."

"Have you heard about this?" said Carah, indicating my mock layout.

"You mean how MB's prostituting her entire *section* to get some glee from the Glee Club?" she said. "Good thing it's completely manipulative and a totally underhanded excuse to meet guys." She hugged my head. "I am *so proud* of you, neighbor."

In my rage I sank to her level of good things. "Good thing you are *so wrong*, Amy," I cried, disentangling myself. "Good thing that is the most *disgusting* thing I have ever heard you say. I will *not* sit here and have the honor of the Glee Club besmirched in my own room."

"Right," she said. "You'd probably like to do the besmirching in one of *their* rooms."

I kicked her.

"There's no need to get *upset* about it, MB," Amy said. "Good thing it's about *time* you grew a pair."

I erased some more lines on the graph paper, with much greater force than necessary.

Amy held her arms upright like Touchdown Jesus. "Ladies and gentlemen, we have achieved puberty!" she yelled.

I took back my ruler.

✳ ✳ ✳

I sat in Notre Dame's music building a few days later, balancing a small tape recorder and a notepad of *Observer* paper on my lap, the only possessor of two X chromosomes in the room. Fifty-five guys stood in sweatshirt-clad ranks on risers before me, tuning. There were two *hours* of it, and when rehearsal adjourned a few of them bounded up to me and asked if I wasn't the Mary Beth Ellis, who wrote for *The Observer*? Really? And I was writing an article on *them*? Would I please be nice?

I stared at dust in floor cracks and said yes, yes, of course, don't worry about it, they were the *Glee* Club, and therefore worthy, and watch for the piece in *The Observer* next week, okay?

I churned out the article in an hour and a half, barely time for me to obsess and compulse over it. I used a framing technique, switching back and forth between an italicized description of the rehearsal I'd attended and an account of the Club's traditions and singing style.

Save. Print. O Lord, the *Gone With the Wind* of feature articles. People would cry, they would *cry*, when they saw me wielding adjectives the likes of these before them.

When I asked the graphics guy who was working that day to scan the Club picture for me so the production tech and I could place it in the layout, he offered to crop it so that I had more room for quotes. I brought him chocolate.

"You know what else I could do?" he said, tearing the wrapper off the Twix bar. "I could fuzz the edges of the picture so it blends into the text."

He tapped a few keys and made the edges fuzzy, and I had never seen such beautiful, transformative fuzz in all my days. "It's so great that you actually care about how this is going to look," I told him.

"I get a dollar bonus every time I do something fancy like that," he said, standing up to make a notation on a chart above the computers.

My production tech and I finished the spread as far as we could. The photographer was late with the stupid photo poll, and the dark room tech even later developing the roll when he finally did deign to appear. Deadline was sitting on my head.

The new features editor came in to check the spread. A brilliantly smiling Lynn had vacated the building about a week ago. "Mary Beth," he said, "this Glee Club thing."

"I know. Doesn't it look *great?* I love how the graphics guy faded the—"

"It's the article. I don't understand it. What's with the italics?"

"Don't understand—"

"When people see italics," he said, as though talking to a very small child who sucked paint chips for lunch, "they stop reading. Rewrite it, okay?"

I stood there, drumming my fingers against the light board. No, *not* okay. I'd already pestered the production tech into a murderous mood, and I was loathe to disturb her further to make a change. The campus, I was certain, would not spin off the planet because the students were wandering the halls in a maw of confusion once they picked up their *Observers* in the morning: "These italics in the features section! I don't get it! I just don't get it! What are we going to *do?*"

And it was late and I was tired, and at nine o'clock in the morning I was scheduled to take an exam for which I had not yet begun to study.

"Those head shots are ready for you," the tech called.

"Thanks," I said, and flounced to the computer to disobey a direct order.

When the heir to Lynn's kingdom saw the finished spread with the italics intact, he threw a fit. I threw a fit right back at him. And walked back to Regina. And threw hard and shattering objects against the walls of 212 until Amy appeared at my door to announce the fact that she was going to kill me.

By next week, "Changing of the Guard", when the campus clubs and organizations phased out the old leaders and phased in the new, was in full swing. The deck reshuffled at the *Observer*—new editor in chief, new SMC editor. Rosalinda, gunning for editor in chief for her senior year, hung in with news. I handed in my letter of intent, a formal statement announcing that I planned to keep my job with all its fabulous, toilet-paper intensive benefits. I needed to stay on the staff to maintain eligibility for my own column as an upperclassman.

The new editor-in-chief, Robert, asked to see me.

He ushered me into his office and closed the door.

"Siddown," he said.

I remained standing.

Robert regarded the life-size cardboard cutout of C-3PO in

the corner of his office for a moment. "We have a problem," he announced.

"I'm so *very* sorry," I said. "It'll never happen again. I won't use italics in my articles anymore—"

"What?" he said.

I exhaled. "Never mind."

He leaned back in his chair. "We appreciate how well you've represented Saint Mary's this semester."

C-3PO stared at me with dead, dead eyes.

"But I don't think it's working out with you as a features editor."

What th— "I... don't understand where this is coming from."

He leaned forward. "Mary Beth," he said, "The other day you locked yourself in the darkroom and refused to come out until everyone agreed to refer to you as 'Rainbow Brite.' People are starting to contact Security."

"Yes. Sorry."

"We need a change where you're concerned."

"Yes. Sorry."

"How would you like an editorial column?"

"Sor—what?"

"We like your writing," he said. "We just don't like you... in *here.*" He waved his arms around.

"Agreed."

"Editorial columnists aren't paid staff members," he warned. "You would lose your paycheck."

"Oh," I said, "and cut back on my Tic-Tac budget?"

Half an hour later I met Madison. Madison was the editorial editor. "Nine hundred words, double spaced, every other week," she said.

I waited for further instruction. "And?"

"And.... other than that, you're on your own." She rushed off to the production office.

I loved Madison.

⁎ ⁎ ⁎

"Hey," I hollered down the hall when I came back to Regina, "I'm home!"

I banged into 212 and found a computer disk. For four years, I never missed a deadline, because somewhere across the street, I knew, was a section editor, attempting to remove her own intestines with a pizza cutter.

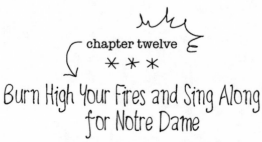

chapter twelve
* * *

Burn High Your Fires and Sing Along for Notre Dame

Two North and I sat in the dining hall, collectively leaning over a Friday *Observer*, reading Bookstore Basketball team names aloud to one another. This was a spring charity tournament sponsored by our brother school, the main point of which was to outwit the other team by mocking one's own. You needed five people and an entry fee and the best team name in the world:

"Pete Rose Would Not Even Bet On Us"

"The Gipper and Four Other Guys Who Will Begin Bombing in Five Minutes"

"We Took More Shots Than That Last Night"

"Four Catholics and One Guy Who *Can* Use Birth Control"

"5'6" and Over Need Not Apply"

"Four Guys Who Still Wonder Why Barney Rubble Never Got His Own Show and One Guy Who Swears He Saw it Once On Cable"

"Top 5 Reasons Why Admissions is Flawed"

I was inspecting a suspicious strand of hair I'd found in a fruit cup I'd inherited from Grace's tray. It was grey. I'm a blonde. Grace had black hair.

I set the fruit aside.

Justine swept up to us and slammed her tray to the table. "Guess what. You," she said, pointing at me, "are going to a dance tonight."

"Guess what. You," I said, pointing at her, "are sadly mistaken."

"Okay, get this," she said, dragging up a chair from another table. We shoved over to make room, turning our trays to vertical. "I'm going to an SYR and my date has a friend whose date fell through. It's kind of an emergency."

"I am not pursuing a college education to act as a social MASH unit."

"I haven't even told you everything yet."

"Oh...I think you have."

"I wish," Justine said sadly, "that you would change your mind."

"Baby, you couldn't change my mind if you whapped me unconscious with a great big stick."

"I just thought," she added, "that you'd like your very first dance to be one sponsored by the Glee Club."

I froze with a forkfull of cottage cheese halfway to my mouth. "It's a Glee Club dance?"

"Whap," said Anne.

Justine nodded. "An SYR. Actually, they call it an SYS— Screw Your Sectionmate—you know, they sing in voice parts—"

Amy snorted.

"— and I have a date all set up for you, MB. You won't have to do a thing but make yourself beautiful, collect your flowers, and have a good time. And you *will*," she concluded, "have a good time."

I began to feel ill, anxiety shoving interest aside. "The hell I will."

"Ten," Kathy said, eyes still on the newspaper.

I had, in the past six months, acquired an unseemly swearing habit. Patty, Kathy, and I were embroiled in a Lenten pact to perform ten push-ups for each transgression. We hated it. It hated us. I dropped to the floor of the dining hall.

"You should've just given up using staples like I did," said Justine.

"Don't do it in *here!*" said Amy. "God!" She hid behind her napkin.

"Ask your big-man singing date if he saw the *Observer* feature you wrote on them," said Anne.

"Oh, *that* eight-hundred-word orgasm," said Carah. She raised her eyes and arms to the ceiling. "'The Glee Club boasts a sparkling concert personality that lusciously complements a variety of music, from Notre Dame football cheers to haunting sacred pieces to beguiling contemporary selections.' Ohhhhhhh!"

I concentrated on the limp honeydew. "I needed to make word count, okay."

Kathy referenced bulls and shit and dove to the floor. "It had to be said," she announced as she resurfaced.

"You're a groupie, and it is *sad*," said Anne.

"Up yours."

"Push-ups!" said Anne.

"That's not cussing," I told her, sipping at my Sprite. "That's just rude."

"Judges?"

"Denied," said Kathy. "It doesn't have four letters."

Justine said, "We have to be at Dillon Hall around nine-thirty, and Juice and I will introduce you to Frances."

I threw down the fork. "Oh, *come on*, Justine!"

"Listen. Juice is an old friend of mine and Frances—well, anyway, just trust me. You'll have fun."

"I can just *imagine* the kind of fun I'll have with a person named Juice and a person named—what is it, Frances?"

She nodded.

"Don't any of these people have normal names?" I retrieved the fork in order to stab at some cottage cheese. "I just don't want to find myself in a... *situation*, that's all."

"Mary Beth is right," said Grace. "I heard the University put the Club on probation for partying too much."

Amy laughed so hard she choked on her Two-Cheese Sandwich Special. "Right. Good thing the National Choirboy Association really knows how to *tear it up*."

"It's true," I told her. "This girl in my poli sci class? She said her roommate's sister's friend told her that when they have parties, they serve that one grain alcohol—what's it called, Everclear? They serve that *without a mixer*. It's not even legal in Indiana. You have to go to Michigan for that sh—stuff."

"I love the dance dress your parents gave you for Christmas," Justine said loudly.

"You're *dying* to wear that dress," said Carah.

"For the right *occasion*, whatever that turns out to be, not some person named after a talking mule. I am not wearing that dress to impress a total and complete stranger."

"Frances could be the right occasion," Carah said.

Justine had a coughing fit.

"YOU DON'T HAVE TO MARRY HIM, MB," said Edmonds to the entire dining hall. "JUST HOOK UP WITH HIM."

"What's Frances like?" Kathy asked Justine.

"You'll like him, MB. He's tall—"

"Oh, well—*sign me up.*"

"He's tall, and his last name is Trenton, and—and—he's in the Glee Club… and…well… he's *Frances*."

"Don't go," said Anne. "You know how you freak out with this stuff. I don't want to see you get hurt." She paused. "Or criminally charged."

"Oh, she's a big girl. She can handle it," said Justine.

"I've got five bucks that says she doesn't handle it," said Kathy.

"Fifteen," said Patty.

Amy slapped the table. "Okay," she said. "Let's make this interesting. Let's set the odds on MB curled in a little ball and crying on the dance floor at…"

I picked up my tray and moved to another table.

Justine followed me. "So what do you think?" she said.

"I'm thinking of moving off-campus."

She played with a piece of lettuce from her salad. "You know what I mean."

I sighed. My OCD had slowed to occasional car-alarm chirps on my subconscious. Hugging Jamey Sotis hello two months earlier had failed, much to my relief, to result in illegitimate Leprechaun babies. Dancing, though—a *dance*, with bodies touching—

"WE CAN'T LET MB CURL HER BANGS FOR THE DANCE, ALL RIGHT? SHE NEEDS TO LOOK TOTALLY DIFFERENT FROM THE WAY SHE USUALLY DOES," Edmonds announced.

"Don't look at them," said Justine. "This is a part of college I don't want to see you miss, all right? Just come with me tonight and we'll all stop bothering you about it."

I stared down at my tray.

"You'll have fun," said Justine.

I stared down at my tray.

"MB?"

"All right," I said.

She clapped her hands. "You're going to have so much fun!"

"Mmm-hmm."

"Trust me." She saw me tapping my fingers on the table. "And don't freak."

I started shredding my hard roll instead. "Right."

"You're freaking *right now*. Stop it. You *will* have a good time." Justine stood up, then placed both hands on the table and leaned over me. "And if you do that push-up thing tonight, I swear to you, I *swear*, I will uncoil your entrails before your very eyes."

"Looking forward to it!" I said brightly.

From the packed table across the dining hall: "The GLEE CLUB! MB has a date with the GLEE CLUB! And suddenly I've found, its members get around...."

I pulled out my student planner and turned to the page for February 9, 1996. "Transfer," I wrote, and went back to shredding the hard roll.

✳ ✳ ✳

"Trenton," I muttered, running my finger down the list of names. "Trenton." I was sitting on the floor of my room after my last class let out, the program from the Glee Club's last concert on my lap. It was open to the page listing the name, major, voice part, and year of graduation for each member.

I found my date amongst the baritones. Trenton, Frances Davidson. Well. So he enjoyed daily beatings as a child. He was a finance major—okay, unlike me, he would have a job after graduation, which was especially good since he was Class of '96 anyway, and...

Class of—

Class of '96... *he was a senior.* My co-pilot for my maiden dating voyage was a twenty-two year old.

"JUSTINE!" I hollered. Oh, the fugly this would bring. "JUSTINE MARIE!"

I stomped to her room and found her placidly studying bio.

"May I help you?"

"A *senior?*" I yelled, slamming the program to her desk. "You fixed me up with a *senior?*"

"So?"

"*So?* My *big sister* is a senior. My sister's *fiance* is a senior. Oh! Oh, *ew!* This is like dating my *brother-in-law!*" I wrung my hands.

"Would you shut up?" she said, shoving me into her beanbag chair. "This is not high school, Mary Beth. Age doesn't matter in college."

"*Nixon!*" I yelled, slamming my fist into the bag. "*Nixon* was president the year he was born! *He was born an entire presidential administration before I was!* "

"That's absurd. The Leprechaun's a senior. You *love* Jamey."

"Jamey doesn't count. I'm not dating Jamey. I doubt he even pees standing up. I think he might have some sort of testosterone defect."

"Mary *Beth*, don't make me smack you."

I sank down amongst the beans, seething.

Justine crouched down to my level. "Now," she said calmly, "are you ready to listen?"

The beans continued to settle around me.

"It does not matter," she said, "that Frances is graduating in three months and you are graduating in three years. It does not matter that he can buy beer and almost rent a car and the most exciting thing you can do with your ID is buy a Powerball ticket. It doesn't even matter that you two are chronologically separated by a White House oath of office."

"Two," I corrected automatically. "Ford."

She dropped her head into her palms. *"Oh* my God. Mary Beth, you have got to calm *down.* This is *college.* People in college date, and people in college sometimes date other people older than they are. He's taking you to a dance. Not a drive-thru wedding chapel. And trust me on this, you—"

"Are going to have a good time," I finished sullenly.

"Yes. Now get out."

I retrieved my program and started stalking back to my room. "And don't—"

"Freak. I know, I know." I stalked the rest of the way to 212. To freak.

A *senior!*

I paced around my room, ducking under my dress, which I had hung from my loft in a last-minute attempt to erase the wrinkles that a magnificent feat of suitcase cramming had put there. How ridiculous was this? I was Dean's list! I was published now! And here I was reduced to—

I was *published.*

I grabbed the student directory. Working on the Glee Club article for *The Observer* hadn't left me without contacts.

I caught one of them in his dorm room, explained the situation, and started pumping.

"You're coming to the SYS? Great. You'll have a good time," he announced.

"Oh crap…"

"Who's your date?" he asked.

"Frances."

"Frances?"

"Yes."

"Trenton."

"Yes."

"Oh."

"What, is there another male under the age of seventy over there with that name?"

"You have never been to a dance before in your whole entire life and somebody fixed you up with Frances Trenton."

"Yes."

He coughed.

I banged the receiver against the wall a couple times. "This is *not funny.*"

"Okay," he said. "You didn't hear this from me. Frances is a good guy, but he's kind of—okay, well, he's..."

Actually a woman? On parole? *Did he have a good personality?* "*What?*"

"Well, he's... he's just Frances."

"Damn you people, I refuse to go out with a person describable only by his first name." Oh, sh—*shoot.* "Excuse me a moment," I said, setting down the receiver. "I have to do ten push ups."

"*What?*"

"I'm back," I gasped into the phone when I'd finished. "You were saying?"

"Frances Trenton," he said, "is the type of person who, if there is no one to talk to, will talk to him*self.*"

"Okay, so I won't have to worry about forcing conversation," I said.

"Forcing conver*sa*tion? My dear, the last time the Club went on tour he wouldn't shut up when the rest of us were trying to sleep on the bus. We had to drug him."

"You *drugged* him?"

"About four sleeping pills, right in his Coke can. He was out for hours. It was the only peace and quiet any of us got that entire trip."

I was going to *kill* Justine. "Fantastic."

"But you'll—"

"Have fun. Yes."

After I hung up I sat there motionless for a few seconds, staring into space. Forget it. Just… forget it. I wasn't ready. Frances Davidson Trenton was just going to have to find himself another date to be screwed by.

I reached for the directory again and started paging from the back. No. Absolutely not. I was not going through with this. My relationship with the Glee Club was just going to have to remain restricted to glowing feature articles and respectful, yet longing, gazing from the theatre seats.

Okay. Good lie, good lie.

Homework.

No. Too pedestrian.

Dead relative?

Too blatant.

What about a violent illness? "Frances (cough, gag), I'm very sorry, but I just can't seem to stem this projectile vomiting." Weak but serviceable.

Trenton, Frances Davidson. Okay. Okay. I punched half the number and tossed the directory in the direction of my desk, in the process jostling my dress to the floor.

I stopped dialing as I bent to pick it up. The black acetate and glitter concoction slid through my fingers like water.

I replaced the receiver.

All right, Frances Davidson Trenton.

But only to wear the dress.

It was unusually warm that day, winter pumping its brakes before coasting into spring. I would, I decided, run the nerves into exhaustion.

I pulled on pink sweatpants and a baseball cap and got halfway down the Avenue before I realized I was wearing one sock.

Four hours later I was climbing the side steps of Dillon Hall. "Justine?" I said. "I'm going to be sick."

Justine, who had downed a Coke spiked with Southern Comfort while Amy was curling her hair, was teetering her way up the stairs ahead of me. "You shoulda taken a shot like I told you. I feel *great.*" We reached the third floor and she very carefully placed a spiked heel on the landing, leaning over the banister. "I'm too high," she announced.

"Congratulations," I said.

"Goooooooood, you're pale!" Justine said when she turned around to watch my progress. "You look like a Clorox bottle with earrings! I mean, you always were albino, but— oh, child! Have a shot. You'll feel better." She pulled me into a double room. "This is the place. Hi, Juice!"

"He lives two floors down," a male voice from within said.

"Sorry. Hugs," Justine said, and continued to drag me down the hall. I scouted the emergency exits.

We found Juice's room. We found Juice. Juice's hair was dyed yellow. I don't mean blonde. I mean... yellow.

"I didn't get you flowers," he greeted Justine.

There was one member of the party missing. "Frances just called," Juice told me. "He said to tell you he's shining his shoes."

Justine screamed. "That is *so great!* Isn't that *great,* Mary Beth? Your date *shines his shoes!*"

"Well, I'm just going to have to let him have his way with me then, aren't I?" I said. I rubbed my arms. "Is anybody else really really cold?"

Juice was pouring vodka into a twenty-four ounce dining hall tumbler. "Nope!" he said.

The door banged open. "Dammit, Juice, I want some alcohol. Justine, how the hell are ya. Hi, you must be Date." He extended a hand. It held a mangled pink rose.

I took it by the fingertips. "Hi. Yes. I mean, thanks."

"Oh, wait! Wait wait wait. Card." He reached into his sock. "Here."

He'd scrawled the entire chorus of "Fire" on the tiny cardboard rectangle. "Um. Thank you."

"Hendrix," said Juice, nodding. "Out*standing*."

Frances raised his eyebrows at me, hands in his pockets. "We're going to have a good time tonight."

✳ ✳ ✳

Apparently the "screw" in "SYR" also doubled as "screwdriver," of which my date had several. He flung an arm over my shoulders as we wove our way down the quad to the campus' Knights of Columbus hall (of *course* it had a Knights of Columbus hall).

"You know, Mary Ellen," he said as I stiffened considerably, "I feel I must warn you...Knights is a concrete slab of a place. Nice and small, but a slab. My brothers and I, though, we'll make it plenty welcoming for you and the lovely Justine here."

"You could have left the flower in Juice's room," the lovely Justine here said.

I shook my head. "I want it with me."

"You *knooooow* what you want outta life!" my date hollered.

I concentrated on the sidewalk. "Your Christmas concert was very good."

"You went to that?"

"I go to all of them."

"Even the ones before football games?"

I didn't answer.

"Every... week?"

"Okay—"

"Ohhhhhh, yes, curious girl. I *thought* I recognized you."

"It's on my way to the Marching Band concert before they step off to march the stadium."

He howled. "On the *other side of campus?*"

"I don't—"

"Wha'd you think of our fall concert? I had a solo in that one."

"Oh!" I darted a glance up at him. "I loved how at the end the director called all the Glee Club alumni in the audience to sing the Alma Mater with you. It was a lovely way to end it."

He leaned into me. "You know what else was lovely?"

I leaned away. "What?"

"The flask we passed around the baritone section."

"On-stage?"

"No better place for it, baby. No better place, I must say."

I saw Justine and Juice stop ahead of us. "The ladies might want to go around," he called back. "One of those South Quad lakes up here."

Melted snow had formed an enormous puddle. When Frances and I reached it, I skimmed the bottom of one silver shoe over the surface of the water. "Lovely."

Justine peered into the depths. "You could hold a regatta in there. Let's go the long way, MB."

"It has *waves*," Juice said.

"Oh please," said Frances. "Pa-*lease. Juice, please.* We are brothers and we are gentlemen." Whereupon he picked me up and sloshed in.

"Okay. Um. This... really isn't necessary...." If I struggled, he'd drop me. If I didn't I would have to stay... like this, in full body contact *with a boy*.

"Oh, honey, honey—this is a *Glee Club* production."

Behind me I heard Justine say, "You don't *have* to..." to her date's evident relief, but when I turned around, Juice was airlifting her over the small lake.

Frances deposited me, unimpregnated, on the other side. He offered me his arm. "Elegance," he said.

✳ ✳ ✳

The Knights building was, indeed, a slab. The basement ceiling was low and the extent of the dance decorations was the crucifix already attached to the wall. Frances' brothers sent up a cheer when we entered, and I shrank into Justine, who shoved me onto the dance floor.

Ten minutes later I found myself staring at the ceiling of the Knights of Columbus building as concerned members of the Notre

Dame Glee Club gathered around me. Frances, with me in one hand and a Miller Genuine Draft in the other, had dropped me in the middle of "Baby Got Back".

"Oh, man, Trenton, your woman's down," one of them said. "You didn't spill any brew, did you?"

"I don't think so," he said with relief. Then he noticed that he was missing a dance partner. "What are you doing on the floor, Mary Ellen?"

"Got the SMC on her back already," a bass announced as he danced by. "Well done, brother."

A teetering Justine hauled me to my feet. "Want to avoid a *situation*, do you?"

"*Shut* up."

Frances hauled me next to him. "Keep it live, baby, keep it live."

"Gentlemen." The president of the Glee Club had temporarily shut down the DJ and shooed everyone in a circle to the edges of the dance floor. "The time has come."

"Schnarenaaaade!" said Justine.

"Okay," said the president. "We'll need soloists. Matt, you take the first verse. I want to hear Bobby over there second. And— Trenton, the last. Ready?"

There was the thin whine of a pitch pipe, then: "Cigarettes and whiskey and wild, wild women, they'll drive you crazy, they'll drive you insane…"

I looked over at Justine, her unfocused eyes; she was missing this synchronized seduction, this night of passion as arranged by Robert Shaw.

The soloists paced the center of the circle as they sang, shaking hands with the other men, hugging the ladies. The hall dropped to complete silence as Frances began his turn around the room.

He began very softly. "Sing out, brother!" somebody yelled from the other side of the room. By the time he'd made his way back to me, Frances was yelling, on-key. "Oh, the temptations of Eve…" He twirled me around and kissed my hand to a testosterone-fueled roar. "I got my shoes wet for this one!" he hollered.

✳ ✳ ✳

As my key found the doorknob in the semi-darkness of the hallway, I discovered a note on my memo board. "MB—A frog or a prince? Come tell me about your wonderful (or terrible) time! I don't care how late it is, my door's unlocked. Anne."

Still cradling my sweetheart rose, a morning-after Miss America, I slipped off my heels and padded down the hall to room 216. "Anne?" I said quietly, pushing the door open.

She stirred in her loft. "Mary Beth? What time is it?"

"Almost three. Sorry I woke you up."

"No, no, I want to know how it —Ow!" She flung a hand over her eyes as she flipped on a light. "Come here so I can see your hair."

I climbed onto her desk and clung to her loft so we were face to face. "That's right, you missed the hair spray explosion. You left for the movie before the girls finished curling the back."

"Oh, MB, you're beautiful."

"Thanks. Amy lent me her WonderBra."

"Did you have fun?"

"I had fun."

"Did he drink?"

I snorted.

"Oh. Did you drink?"

"I'm coherent, aren't I?"

She yawned. "Did he kiss you?"

I leaned my forehead against the loft, smiling into the wood.

"Oh *really.*"

"On top of the head, while we were dancing," I amended.

"I'm glad you had a nice time."

"Me too. Go back to sleep. I'm gonna take a shower." I jumped down from her desk, my nyloned feet dropping silently to the carpet. I collected my rose and headed for the hallway.

"A *shower?* At this time of night?"

I clutched at my rose. "Yeah. All the hairspray."

"MB, look at you." She propped herself up on one elbow. "You're a woman who's been sung to."

"I... need to get out of this makeup," I said, shutting the door, leaving only moonlight to break the darkness of her room.

chapter thirteen
* * *

Roommates

The campus of a women's college is a dangerous place in the spring, for this is the era of room selection.

A disturbing majority of female college graduates, when asked about room selection, had they the ability to point to an X-ray of their very souls, would indicate a long, dark fracture and say something along the lines of, "Yeah. Right there, junior year, when Jill and I decided to get a double room and Renee thought we were all going to stay in the triple."

Room selection is the halfway-point of adult female relationships, the social wind tunnel between picking teams on the grade school playground and choosing bridesmaids. The very broaching of the topic requires the delicacy of negotiation with a roof-jumper who has a hostage and a gun and a bomb and the President of the United States' kitten under his arm, for room selection exposes the horrors of splitting up the female pack. Suddenly a troupe consisting of four or six women has to parcel itself out two by two, and God help the group that consists of an uneven number. You've seen young women negotiate the universe, the mall and the candle shops and the bookstore cafes, in these groups. We don't even go to the *bathroom* by ourselves, let alone decide in pairs on a living space and settle out who gets the medicine cabinet that doesn't stick without stabbing backs and hurting feelings and in general ending the world.

This is not a yearly trauma exclusive to Saint Mary's. It is one thing to stay up until four in the morning discussing with a friend whether or not the couch you're currently sitting on actually exists. It's quite another to sleep with your head four inches away from her alarm clock for a year. I think there's a reason why the best roommate my sister ever had at her big state college was the randomly assigned zoology major she met on move-in day. ("Get the good bed, get the *good bed!*" my mother hissed at her.) Room selection means choosing sides, which, in Woman World, is *simply* not done in front of one another's backs. I saw friendships destroyed during room selection; objects thrown, futons split. It's saddest of all, when it comes to that, for why should the futon suffer a broken home simply because its two mommies can't get along?

A large portion of Two North had decided to stay put in Regina and was wary when Justine, Anne, and I decided to make tracks for Holy Cross Hall, which was situated on the edge of campus but at least offered enough space to be able to open a book without balancing the desk out the window first. I couldn't wall-walk in Holy Cross, which was a former classroom building; instead, I log-rolled or somersaulted down the wide hallways, spine cracking against the floorboards.

It wasn't quite the same.

The problem was, as sophomores, we didn't have room selection numbers high enough to score singles in such a popular hall. If I wanted to live in Holy Cross, I'd have to have a roommate.

This was when I was young and cocky and thought myself tolerable. Justine had already brokered a roommate deal with another Regina resident, and I'd heard that Grace told Amy who'd told Edmonds who'd screamed to Patty that Anne was also inter-ested in living in Holy Cross.

Anne, like me at the beginning of my freshman year, wasn't tremendously interested in the dating circuit, and plus she owned a refrigerator with an automatic defrost setting, so I approached her and proposed room marriage. "This is a good match," I said. "We both need total quiet to study, we have a couple classes together, and it's not like either of us are going to have to work out deals on men in the room."

This conversation took place, however, perhaps two days after the Great Frances Awakening. Directly after that, with the help of the wondrous fluvoxamine, I rocketed through social puberty in about a semester, in the space of that time hitting for what was known as the Glee Club Grand Slam: a date with at least one member of each voice part. The bass came last.

Two North knew better. They saw the way my extracurricular campus life was going, in the sense that I was actually acquiring one, and, of course, they'd *met* me. They started a pool. The odds of one of us asking for a dorm transfer by Fall Break were running at Secretariat levels.

"You are going to *kill* each other," Carah said, who knew well what happens when you put two German Catholics in an enclosed space.

I pished upon her concerns.

"Oh, pish," I said. "We're grown women and good friends. I don't see why this shouldn't work."

For about eight hours, it did. On our first night as roommates, Anne wanted to turn in early and I was eager to read through some of my new textbooks—shut *up*—and so I took a little can of Pringles and some bottled water in the hallway, stretched my legs out, and happily crunched and read in the semidarkness.

The next morning the sun broke over our slumbering little faces and we woke up and congratulated each other on how well this was going, and then I accidentally locked Anne out of the room. This happened perhaps five billion more times.

And *then* I got a boyfriend, whom she hated, possibly because she was jealous, definitely because he was an unmitigated ass; and she got a social conscience, which I mocked. She was blazingly active in all sorts of volunteer clubs and Catholic social thought classes and money-collecting, all of which were admirable, but these inevitably involved *people*, whereas I was intent upon saving the world by typing smack about Ohio State over at *The Observer* office. Soon all we had in common was our mailbox keys.

The political fissure between us shook and spread; the weathered walls of Holy Cross were further battered by our sometimes ideological, sometimes idiosyncratic, but always idiotic, fights. One night a stray cigarette started a small fire on the third floor. We clattered down the wooden staircase in our nightgowns as the fire alarm wailed, still screaming about the constitutionality of the death penalty.

At this point in my life I conducted arguments via the highly constructive technique of slamming doors and slapping things. It never came to physical blows with Anne, but my hands did touch typewriter keys: Once I quoted a malapropism of hers in an *Observer* column, and although I did not put her name to it, on the day the piece ran, her numb hurt frosted the very windowsills.

I thought liturgical dancers were an abomination to man and Church; she *was* one. She felt that Boyfriend The First invaded her space; her continued and studied temerity in refusing to see every single thing my way infuriated me. I went to bed just as she was stirring to her alarm for morning Mass. When it was peaceful I liked to show affection and repentance by petting her hair as she worked at her desk; she found this, for some reason, irritating.

The rest of Two North, watching afar from the safety of Regina, lowered the odds.

It was one of those no-fault roommate wars, in which we shared equal blame for the boiling pot of angst that was 251 Holy Cross. I was sarcastic, thoughtless, opinionated, and quick to anger; Anne, for her part, over and over again committed the mortal sin of continuing to exist. "Thanks for always being there"—this is what I wrote in a card to her during the Christmas of our freshman year. And now, now that we were confined to the same four walls, I was constantly furious because... she was... *always there.*

Two or three times a week I shaved my legs in the middle of the room, foam in one hand and a wad of paper towel in the other, seething. Did she have to fill out her student teacher journals *now*? Bizarre! I'd glare at the back of her head and bend over my dry legs again, scrape scrape scrape.

We never got to the point of property destruction, although Two North's over-under on combined damages exceeding four grand was impressive.

One night, just before Thanksgiving, late for dinner due to a fight with Boyfriend The First and terrified bloodless over a poli sci exam the next day, I slapped my room keys down at a table containing Anne, Kathy, and Justine.

"Where've you been?" Kathy said.

Anne concentrated on her chicken a la king.

"Never mind," I said, but was suddenly one percent more cheerful now that there was chicken on the horizon.

I went to the steam tables. Out of chicken. Have some creamed corn instead.

I slammed together a salad and returned to the table in tears.

Justine put down a half-peeled orange in alarm. "What? What?"

"They are *out... of... chicken!*"

I flung a napkin in Anne's general direction and sobbed off.

The day after the Chicken Outburst, I put in a quiet request for a single at the Housing Office. The waiting list was four pages long. Sophomores dominated.

"Tried to live with a friend, did you?" said the receptionist.

"Yeah, well—" I signed my name as legibly as possible.

"Oh, Ellis," said the secretary, picking up a phone. "I was asked to call an Amy Wilson in Regina if you showed up here."

When room selection came around again, Anne moved in with Carah, who, although she could get along with a premenstrual wombat, I refused to take on as a roommate. I refused to take on *anybody*. I visited the two of them a few times, there in LeMans Hall. The room was decorated in a cool green, pictures of Carah's year abroad in Ireland softly blending with Anne's Shaker bedspread. I moved to another dorm entirely, into a single, and have never inflicted myself upon a roommate since, goldfish included.

The only snapshot I can find from the end of sophomore year is one my father took of me with just-permed hair, bending over a half-stuffed suitcase of tee shirts, a riot of finals notes scattered on the polished wooden floor. It looked as if my closet had just thrown up. My roommate is nowhere to be seen.

Anne immersed herself in her early education major, and I disappeared into writing workshops. I saw her around campus now and then, mostly when she was collecting donations for earthquake victims or sexually abused seahorses or children born without eyebrows or whatever. I have a few pictures of us together at Two North reunion parties. But only a few.

The April before we graduated, I found a corners-bent birthday card in my mailbox. I opened it, confused; my birthday is in January.

"Found this in my storage locker. I was too mad to give it to you at the time," the note at the bottom read. "I forget why. Love, Anne."

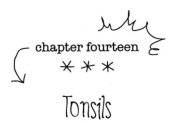

chapter fourteen

* * *

Tonsils

At the state college my sister attended, the infirmary was referred to as "Kill 'Em and Hide 'Em." "My nose is running and I'm sneezing a lot," Julie would say during her phone calls home, "but I am *not* going to Kill 'Em and Hide 'Em."

I was confident that at my college, my tiny, Catholic, close-knit women's college, I would never have any qualms about finding medical comfort, especially after the first itemized bill arrived from Saint Mary's and we discovered that a compulsory charge of $90 had been tacked on to my tuition for "Health Services." "If you feel *one smidge* less than in perfect health," my father said, "and that includes a hangnail— you get your butt into that doctor's office."

"What about hangovers?"

"Well, *then* we want you to suffer," said my mother. "But for ninety dollars a semester, I want to see at least a lung transplant."

Even so, I didn't have much opportunity to visit Health Services my freshman year, except to write it a check for $6.95 worth of generic antibiotics to cure a body-wracking cough and runny nose which was diagnosed as "an upper respiratory infection, or maybe bronchitis, or possibly mono."

A few weeks later Amy took a trip to the infirmary with a headache, upset stomach, and fever. She also returned with a bottle and a diagnosis of "an upper respiratory infection, or maybe bronchitis, or possibly mono." Pretty much, if you showed up to Health Services with your femur bone protruding from your thigh in jagged bits, the nurse on call would immediately swing into the Health Services Emergency Procedure of taking your temperature and pronouncing you felled by an upper respiratory infection. Or maybe bronchitis. Or possibly mono.

In the first semester of my sophomore year, I began to lose the aptitude to carry on certain essential faculties such as swallowing. I had to take ten minutes to embolden myself enough to even try, and when I actually managed to get the spit down, my entire body convulsed and my face squinched up.

This entertained Anne for hours. It was her new social activity. She would call people. "Get over here! You've gotta see this! Mary Beth's going to swallow!"

Soon, however, she tired of watching me suffer. "I think," she said as I lay in my loft, exhausted from my latest swallow, "that it's time to go to the infirmary."

I shook my head. No. Not until I was actually having out-of-body experiences. "I'll be fine after I sleep for a while," I managed to whisper. "I want to finish watching this show first."

"Mary Beth," she said, "the television isn't on."

An hour later I was sitting in the Health Services offices with a thermometer crammed in my mouth. The nurse was checking my files. "I see you came in here last semester with an upper respiratory infection," she said.

She came at me with a tongue depressor.

"Hmmm," she said. "I'll be right back."

I was left to stare at a large color chart entitled "STDs: Their Transmission and Symptoms".

Another nurse entered, accompanied by Nurse #1. She also stabbed around my throat with a tongue depressor. "Hmmm," she said, both of them leaving. "Don't go anywhere." I sank back against the examining table. I had a fever of a hundred and two and no way of swallowing. Where, exactly, did they think I would go? The World Figure Skating Championships?

Still another nurse came in. "Open up."

I opened.

"Hmmm," said Nurse The Third. "I think the doctor better take a look at this."

The receptionist had followed her. "Can I see?"

Everybody left again, presumably to invite the students currently in the waiting room to conduct their own inspections at their leisure.

"Dr. Doctor will be in to see you in a minute," one of the nurses said.

I hugged my knees to my chest. It was a good life, there in the Joseph Heller novel.

I took up staring at the STD chart again and had gotten as far down the alphabet as syphilis when Dr. Doctor made his grand entrance with yet another tongue depressor.

"You know, there's a lot of upper respiratory infections going around," he said, staring into my left ear with a pen light.

"Shocking."

"Bronchitis and mono, too," he added, tapping my glands. A searing pain shot through my jaw when he came to the area surrounding my right tonsil.

"Oh," he said, "did that hurt?"

I removed my fingernails from the flesh of his arm and nodded.

"Well now," he said. "This just might be a *severe* upper respiratory infection."

He got out the tongue depressor. I opened.

"Hmmm," he said.

Dr. Doctor left and a nurse returned ten minutes later with— not to alarm me or anything—a Saint Mary's security guard. What was this about? A citation for developing tonsillitis in a non-Upper Respiratory Infection Zone? "Hey," I said, "hey. It was *not* my idea to pry that boot off that car. I think you need to consider—"

"We're sending you to Memorial Hospital to see an ENT specialist," the nurse told me. "You might require an overnight stay."

"But it's chicken and dumplings night in the dining hall," I said.

"Can I see your throat?" said the security guard.

At the hospital complex, I was left to sit in a waiting room and stare at an aquarium for forty-five minutes and listen to my tonsils throb. Two of the fish, I noted, were floating at the top of the tank.

They put me in an examining room with enormous Plaster of Paris ears and brochures with titles such as "Doctor, Tell Me About My Adenoids" and "Snoring: When It's Just Not Funny Anymore." He had a Notre Dame diploma on his wall, which made me feel a little better, until I noticed that it was for a Bachelor of Arts. Dr. Doctor had sent my throat to a man who spent his undergraduate years analyzing *Moby Dick*.

The doctor came in, and "Hmmmm"ed, and whipped out a needle, and started draining the infection. At this point he recognized that what I really needed at that particular moment was small talk.

"So," he said, as I decided that death was highly underrated, "did you see the Air Force game on Saturday?"

"I'm finished," he announced cheerfully, as if he had just polished my shoes instead of inflicting the most disgusting medical procedure of my entire life, and I include in this statement the time my sister threw up in my hair. "How are you doing?"

I bent over an expectorate bowl. They hadn't told me, in my theology classes, that evil tastes and looks like this.

They pushed me back to the Security car in a wheelchair and handed me my backpack, discharge papers, and, best of all, a great big bag of federally regulated medication.

My favorite was the codeine. I remember taking it; I remember not long afterward fearing things like my pillowcase and angry cole slaw.

In addition to colleges, the Catholic Church, incidentally, also runs hospitals.

chapter fifteen

✷ ✷ ✷

Shots

The problem was, I wanted one of the plastic cups. They had "University of Notre Dame Alumni-Senior Club" printed on one side and the 1997 football schedule printed on the other. The *season* had been terrible, but the cup commemorating it was sweet, and here it was my twenty-first birthday and I wanted something overblown and boozy and brother school-ish to remember it by.

But you had to buy a drink to get the cup, so I selected rum and Coke, for the sole reason that ordering it was potentially less humiliating than striding up to the eighty year old man behind the bar and announcing, "I'd like Sex on the Beach, please." It turned out that rum and Coke would have been more aptly named "Battery Acid and Coke" or "Windshield Wiper Fluid and Coke", for all the flavor the rum added, but I downed it anyway, because, you see, I could.

I laid my cheek against Randal's shoulder. He was also turning twenty-one today, having entered the world five hours ahead of me. ("How," a friend who was heavily into astrology once asked when I told her this, "do you *stand* each other?" We turned twenty-one, that's how.)

"Isn't it *great* how we can celebrate our birthdays without getting wasted?" I said. I'm using tonight as my lead for my editorial about the need for alcohol-free dorms. Aren't we *terrific?* I love you, Randal."

"I'm not Randal," he said.

The actual Randal was approaching with my stadium jacket. "Let's go back to the dorm," he said.

"I hate the shuttle," I announced.

"I know," he said, disengaging me from the Domer formerly known as Randal.

Walking had suddenly become far more difficult than usual. "Randal," I said, slapping at his arm. "Randal, I'm *drunk!*"

"I know," he said, guiding me towards the winter air.

"But I don't *drink!*"

He pushed my hood up over my eyes. "I know."

"I just wanted one of the cups!"

"Door's this way."

Well—this was just *terrible*. I was famous for holding my non-liquor. In October of my freshman year I had attended a pep rally with Amy and about seventy of her closest male confidants from Keenan Hall, and I'd hurled myself into the off-rhythm chanting and clapping with my usual...okay...me-ness. Then I bid Amy and her harem good night as they set off for the nearest dorm party to discover more euphemisms for her "Ways To Say Drunk!" door sign.

The following day, Amy got a phone call from one of her gentleman escorts.

"I need to talk to you about your blonde friend from the rally on Friday," he said.

"Mary Beth," she clarified.

"Yeah. Aren't you concerned about her?"

"Huh?"

"Didn't you notice how incredibly smashed she was?"

"Mary *Beth?*"

"I don't have anything against drinking, but she was so *loaded*. I mean, she must have started pounding as soon as her classes were over."

"Mary BETH?"

"You need to talk to her, Amy. Tell her to pace herself next time."

"MARY BETH? She doesn't *drink!*"

"Amy, you are in denial. Face your friend's problem. You have to *help* her."

But now—well, now the editorial lead was shot to hell and I'd probably get kicked off the Alcohol Education Council and why was the stadium moving?

Randal, meanwhile, had found a new science experiment. "This is great," he said. "I've been on the Alcohol Intervention Team for two whole years and now I finally get to see what happens *first hand.* "

"Congratulations," I said, unzipping my coat and flinging it in the general direction of Saint Mary's. "I don't need this any more."

"It's ten degrees out here," he said, chasing after it. "Don't move."

Not a problem.

I had to find a bathroom. "Why did they put the toilets so far apart around here?"

"I'll take you to LaFortune," he said.

"I have to pee."

"Don't go here."

"That's the name of a country song, right? You know? Who sings that? You know, that one guy? Who *is* that guy? With the cowboy hat?"

"Where are your gloves? Can you feel your hands?" he wanted to know.

"I can't feel *anything.*"

"Studies have shown," Randal said as he gently pried my fingers from one of North Quad's bike racks, "that those who are inebriated for less than twenty minutes, especially if they are females, will—"

"Where's my cup? Don't lose my awesome cup."

"Screw the cup."

"Screw *you.*" I sank to my knees as my dinner threatened an encore. "Randal, am I going to die?"

"I don't think so." He grabbed my hair in one handful, holding it away from my face. "Happy birthday."

"Back atcha," I said, and proceeded to throw up on North Dining Hall.

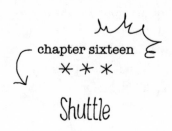

chapter sixteen
✳ ✳ ✳

Shuttle

A shuttle runs between Saint Mary's and Notre Dame. It's a bus, really, stopping at all SMC dorms and most major points of Notre Dame interest, but I refused to refer to it as such. You take the *bus* to stupefying jobs in cubicle burial grounds and have to sit next to people who insist upon conducting conversations with the exhaust fumes. You take a *shuttle* into space, to the airport, and in general exactly where you want to go.

The shuttle was itself a college student, appearing when it felt like it and shutting down completely on the weekends. I did a lot of running after it while cursing, a pattern broken occasionally by futile waiting for it, while cursing.

On some routes the shuttle wound its way to Married Student Housing, a crackerbox, shoved-out-of-the-way Notre Dame apartment complex close to neither campus but featuring, as compensation, an unparalleled view of the Bob Evan's on Route 33. There was always a great deal of loud exhaling when the shuttle turned towards Married Student Housing; it would mean at least a ten-minute delay to whichever campus one was attempting to access, and—let us be honest—whichever new occupant climbed on board there was ineligible for the SYR dating pool anyway.

I lived on the silver whining thing, what with my co-exchange classes and *Observer* work, and, in later years, the boy. There was often a boy.

There was one consistent boy for three years. Randal really wasn't a bad boyfriend, as boyfriends go; a starter boyfriend, low mileage, but bad shocks and a wicked shimmy when you tried to take him on the marriage highway. I got a lot of flowers and hugs, but he said things like "I just don't understand why more people aren't fans of professional wrestling," and when parietals came, he was often suddenly overcome with a wave of exhaustion, forcing me to walk solo in the dark to the nearest shuttle stop or with my arm linked through the elbow of one of his pitying friends. Once he called me a bitch. Once I climbed off the shuttle and directly into a bottle of Schnapp's because he flipped me off in the middle of a fight over U.S. involvement in Kosovo.

Other, normal couples fight about money and exes and perceived slights of attention; at Saint Mary's, in 1997, I fought about Kosovo.

That, and the whole... *priest* situation.

Randal was thinking of becoming a priest, you see. He was a math major, but wanted to be a theology major, and then a priest. He loved nothing more than serving Mass at the Basilica, crew cut solemn above the altar, server's alb brushing the tops of his cowboy boots.

Randal was from Texas.

He grew up in a largely Protestantized background, and sudden immersion in the Catholic Disneyland that is the Notre Dame–Saint Mary's nexus (Parietalsland! NoBaconBitsOntheSalad BarInLentland! OpportunityForMassSeventeenTimesaDayland! GrainAlocholland!) was a warming shock to his Southern system. Mass was his crack.

College itself was mine. By this point, I was inhaling Saint Mary's and exhaling Notre Dame and circulating the campii through my very platelets. It was my distinct impression that the world ceased to exist at the far borders of Saint Mary's, and unless you sat beside me in sweatpants at 10 PM Rosary services, unless you slammed screamingly up against me at the pep rallies and balanced the entire Robert Browning section of the Saint Mary's library in your arms... you *just* didn't get me. You never would.

So I hung in with Randal, who did all these things, and therefore *got me*, and as an added bonus was fairly OCD-accepting ("You're *not pregnant*, okay?" he would say as I rolled up in a dirty corner of his dorm room rather than sit on a bed in which he had been sleeping.) I folded my arms and stared into his pending priesthood.

He considered my writing, however, about as amusing as I found the whole idea of shipping him off to seminary.

"I don't make you laugh, do I," I said two weeks into the relationship.

"Not really."

I was silent for a while. So... if I wasn't entertaining, what in the world was there to like about me? The constant secret handwashing? Mmmmmm yeah, boys dig that.

"Then why," I said, "are you here?"

That made him laugh.

One night I sat waiting for him in Notre Dame's Student Union, studying *Thirteen Days* and a Styrofoam cup of cookies and cream cappuccino while a Damer sat at the next table reading my column in *The Observer.* It was Acoustic Night, and some guy wearing a baseball hat on backwards sat plucking a guitar, mourning into the microphone about how very very difficult his life was, here in Catholic Disneyland with his khakis and his baseball cap. I kicked one leg against my backpack and felt collegiate and highlighted my book and pretty much considered this the best day of my whole entire life.

Randal blew in, bringing the ten-below wind chill factor with him. I tugged at his arm, pointing to the student next to us. "Sweetie, look! She's reading *my column.*"

He nodded, lips pressed together, and looked around at Backwards Hat Guy. "It's so *loud* in here," he said. "Let's go."

Randal delighted in thurifer duties at the Basilica. The thurifer was in charge of the incense, the golden cage on the end of a long clanking chain. Boy did he love incense.

I stood quietly at the back of the church one Sunday morning as he folded one arm against the rough white linen of his alb, bowing to the altar, the priest, the congregation, tolling the metal cask. Smoke curled between us, lingering its way to the ceiling. It almost hid the fact that in his every aspect—arms, eyes, wrists, his very fingernails—was a peace I never saw when he looked at me.

I yanked on a heavy wooden door and fled the Basilica, which takes being a Basilica very seriously. It pretty much brought in God the Father as its interior decorator, with pillars dripping in gold, fields of stars on the ceiling, and a Bernini altar—the only one of its kind, of course, on the entire continent. The steeple is high. The bricks are yellow. They were formed from the very Indiana clay on which I stood.

I kicked the Basilica.

Then I sucked in a few breaths and went back inside so as not to miss Communion.

Where I came from, "So... what's your Confirmation name?" was a legitimate pick-up line and when you met someone new, an initial assignation of class consisted of discerning which parish the person attended. Randal had none of this. Randal thought the Campus Ministry's Living Stations of the Cross was a wonderful thing. And yet when I attended the same event, I practically rolled my eyes into Canada when we were asked to join hands with our neighbors and recite the Our Father. I looked at my friend Flip next to me and said, "Because I have only the highest respect for you, I am going to stand right here and not even *try* to hold your hand." He and I exchanged a liturgically bonding nod instead.

Randal, he *lifted his arms up* at the end of the Our Father.

Whenever I saw him do this, I commanded myself to think of finals week in our sophomore year, when my grandmother died and he visited my professors to ask for an extension on my term papers and tests. Then when he put his arms back down, I would nestle into his shoulder, and he'd rest his hand on my opposite hip, and we'd kneel together before Communion.

"And just how Catholic would you like me to be, exactly?" I would say to the Virgin Mary as she stood atop Notre Dame's Golden Dome. That's her up there, you know—when stitched in yellow thread on the Official Licensed Product tag of my brother school's football merchandise (Fightin' Irish Liquid Hand Soap, getcha some!) it looks like a lumpy spire, but no, it's Mary, eyes on us all the time.

Her right hand is raised. It points directly down the Avenue. Saint Mary's helped raise the money to build the whole affair, I read once, pure gold leafing and all, before Rockne, before the failed merger, before me or Two North or Randal or the big silver shuttle had even been thought of. I spent many hours at Notre Dame's Grotto shrine behind the Basilica pondering this, the converging, the specter of my boyfriend in a Roman collar when I had prayed my entire life for an increase in priestly vocations. You can twirl a Rosary around all you want, but there's no avoiding the spiky metal crucifix hanging at the beginning and the end of it.

You should have seen the pictures of the martyred saints in the picture books I read in church as I grew up. St. Sebastian: Crammed full of arrows. St. Lucy, toted her own eyes around in a dish. Agatha? The Romans chopped her boobs off. Dedicate your own life to God, yes, okay, I supposed I would give my boobs for Jesus. But nobody ever said anything about forfeiting the life of my first love.

✳ ✳ ✳

When we were first dating, Randal and I arranged for him to get on the shuttle at Notre Dame and for me to board at Saint Mary's. We would ride to Married Student Housing and disembark, for from there it was only a short walk to a fantasy dinner date at the Bob Evan's on Route 33. But the shuttle I expected him to arrive on didn't show, so I scurried on to the next one to come along; perhaps

I could still find him at the Grotto stop. And as we chugged down the Avenue, I saw a second shuttle, making an opposite circuit, and through the window, staring, horrified, was Randal, heading very much in the opposite direction.

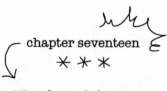

chapter seventeen
✳ ✳ ✳

The Sweet Science

There was plastic orange nacho cheese congealing to the plastic container next to my foot; I nudged it away. "The sweet science," my friend Davy said, pounding one fist into the other. "All reflexes and technique."

Two of the scientists were out in the ring that very moment, one slapping the other upside the head with the hard-pillowed fist of his glove. Gold trunks sagged into slack blue ropes. Blunt exhales, muted thuds.

"Beat him like a rented whore, Mikey!" a voice roared from the other side of the arena.

"You missed it," I said to Davy, reclining against my backpack. "While you were in the bathroom some freshman fell completely on his buttcrack. Feet went right out from under him."

"No kidding." He threw his cap on the ground to pull on a maroon sweatshirt. "Uppercut?"

I pulled at a hangnail. "Untied shoelace."

Such things happened at the Notre Dame Bengal Bouts.

Davy snorted, smoothing back his hair and replacing the hat. "Somebody needed to tell that kid not to drink before he got in the ring." I nodded, eyes on the ring.

"Was there bleeding?" he said after a moment's reflection.

"Nah."

His narrow shoulders draped briefly in disappointment. "Where's Randal?"

"Didn't want to come," I said, tapping my Saint Mary's ring against Randal's high school one, heavy on my right hand. The click was metallic, textured.

Above us, the referee has halted the bout. A first aid worker in bright red snapped a rubber glove over his wrist, clambered through the ropes, and stalked the canvas on his hands and knees, a lick of flame on a ricecake sea. Davy wanted to know which weight class was fighting.

"We're up to the 185's," I said, watching the first aid worker gingerly lift a tiny pearl of an object from the canvas between his thumb and forefinger. He handed the tooth over the ropes to the ring doctor, who cradled it in terrycloth, steam from the iceblock next to his elbow floating above the ring like incense. The referee raised the glove of the winner.

Davy poked at me. "Which class is your friend in again?"

"Charlie's a heavyweight," I said, my voice thudding like the blows in the elevated square. I'd already been here an hour and a half, and I'd probably remain for at least another two. I could feel the sharp edge of cardboard against my left arm. The ten dollar Bengal Bouts ticket—a calm Colorado blue, good quality paper— peeked from my jacket pocket, and I shoved it out of sight. Ten whole dollars—that equaled about two hours at my campus video store job of renting Monty Python movies to shower-shoe-clomping brothers and sisters in the Notre Dame family who yelled at me because we did not stock *Chasing Amy*.

Six weeks now I'd been seeing Charlie drag late into the *Scholastic Magazine* editorial board meetings in the basement of the dining hall, cheeks flushed, slow-moving. Editors-in-chief weren't built for sparring. "Seriously, you guys, I need to unload these tickets," he said after last Thursday's meeting, to no avail. "The money's for the mission in Bangladesh, and all."

I'd planned to donate a hearty good-luck punch on the shoulder. Didn't owe him any more; he was just another student editor-in-chief in the long, long line of student editors-in-chief I'd lowered my eyes to for the past two years. Simply... there.

After the entertainment editor and the managing editor filed out, I looked up from packing up my books to see his awkward torso hunched over one of the computers, a sports layout flickering on the screen before him.

"Are you nervous about your match?" I said to break the mechanical hum of the hard drive, slinging my backpack over my right shoulder, fiddling with one of the straps after it settled there. The dining hall air was tinged with the sharp, piled-on odor of the meals upon meals that had been prepared above our heads.

He turned, adding to the first non-editorial, one-on-one conversation we'd ever had. "Nervous, excited, both."

"Well, don't get your head bashed in, OK?" I said, checking my watch.

He hesitated, then pulled his glasses away from his face. "I got a black eye three days ago."

I approached to inspect the faded swirl of green and callow yellow that circled his left eye. He squinted against the harsh fluorescence of the ceiling. "Oh, ow," I said, cupping his right cheek to tilt his head away from the bluish stare of the computer screen for a better look. "*There* is a war wound."

The eyepieces of his glasses disappeared again into his brown hair. "It doesn't hurt, though."

I pushed a stray strand of hair behind my ear. And bought three tickets. One for me. One for Davy, who applauded violence in any way, shape, or form. And one for my boyfriend Randal, who absolutely hated boxing.

Charlie's glasses were off again now, hair hidden by his helmet. His opponent was sleeker, taller. I jabbed Davy. "He's up," I told him. Next to me, the victor of the previous bout, dripping and quivering, sagged against the steel staircase leading to the upper bleachers, using the handrails for support. Head bowed, arms shining. His girlfriend snapped a picture. Davy resumed his discussion of next Saturday's hockey game with the guy sitting next to him.

I slouched into my sweatshirt and faced front. The abandoned ringside seats scattered before me; huge voids in the bleachers stared down from above. Charlie tapped gloves with his opponent, the contact silent to me. I hollered encouragement to him, well aware that he couldn't hear me for the helmet and the clamor of the bell.

His head slammed back again and again; he wavered, dodged, swung. The referee pulled him aside for eight counts, checking his eyes, tapping him on the shoulder. Charlie bounced in place, nodding. Across the ring his opponent watched, slashing at air.

"Go for the head, Charlie," Davy yelled on my behalf, then returned to hockey talk.

Three rounds it lasted, my thin soprano slicing through the arena, Charlie's steps and jabs heavier and heavier as the lights beat down.

"Stay on your feet, stay on your feet," I called, wishing someone had screamed that at me the last time I had been sweating, spotlit, and tired— an intramural basketball game that had meant nothing at all in the grand scheme of the Honor and Glory of Sport, but had seemed awfully important as I dribbled, guarded, pivoted for forty godawful minutes.

A final ring of the bell; Charlie removed his helmet, head fluttering for an instant to rest against the top rope. He wiped his face, took his place to the referee's right. The announcer held up a gold card and yanked the microphone cord over the ropes.

"He was pulverized," I said to Davy, who nodded.

The judges' decision was unanimous; Charlie stared above my head as his opponent's glove was raised. I hopped down from the bottom bleacher as a trainer untaped his gloves. Charlie's three roommates streamed from the upper decks towards the exit. Miller time.

He dragged past me, gloves in hand. I waved; Charlie squinted in my direction but kept moving.

I caught up, embracing his damp arms and chest. "You really came? Thanks for being here," he said, off guard but grateful, his free hand sweeping around me and landing at the place on my back where my bra fastened.

"Way to hang in there." I pulled back, brushing against one of the rivers of sweat pouring down his face before darting back to my seat beside Davy. The editor in chief melted away from the artificial sun of the ring lights.

I mopped my face on the sleeve of my sweatshirt and crouched down in the tinny darkness next to Davy, who said nothing.

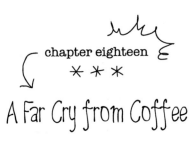

chapter eighteen

A Far Cry from Coffee

f I had the dating mentality of a twelve and a half year old when I first came to college, by the time I was on my second boyfriend I was maybe seventeen. And seventeen-year-olds do some stupid, stupid things.

They cheat on their boyfriends.

With a seminarian.

While the boyfriend is out of town, teaching underprivileged children.

One summer I stayed on campus to work for Saint Mary's Office of Special Events, doing decidedly unspecial work for the camps and seminars that took over the dorms from May until August, because I wished to experience the fun and activity of the academic year minus the actual academics. This turned out to be an excellent plan, if you didn't consider the fact that I forgot that when the academic year goes, the students go too, taking the fun and activity with them.

So I wound up friendless, shuttleless, and foodless in un-airconditioned South Bend for three months, and was paid minimum wage for beating cheerleader campers with their Spirit Sticks to get them to stop overloading the dorm elevators and explaining to Junior Summer Bible Seminar students that while it was very commendable to want to get close to Jesus, He probably didn't spend much time on the roof of the library.

The best part of the job was when I got to change the white plastic letters on our "WELCOME TO SAINT MARY'S COLLEGE" entrance sign. The day the Elderhostel participants were due to arrive, I spelled out "HOURLY RATES AVAILABLE."

I also had the honor of working out in Regina's indoor pool with a pack of eighty-year-old Carmelite nuns on a spiritual retreat, transporting approximately eight thousand oscillating fans from one side of the campus to the other, and—this was the best use of my half-earned degree of all—digging through dining hall garbage in search of a cheerleader's retainer.

I was in that pool a lot, hair floating to the surface, arms raised to the ceiling as I bicycled my legs in the deep end, sucking in chlorinated air. But much as I enjoyed bobbing around in green water with old wet nuns, I was floundering about for a safe, sympathetic source of male advice regarding my rapidly disintegrating relationship with Randal. How provincial, I thought, that Marco had stayed for the summer too.

I'd met Marco about a month before I began dating Randal, in a Notre Dame theology class; we sat next to one another and he spoke all kinds of languages and was a Rhodes scholar and a seminarian and I looked sideways at him and thought "Sail on, Father What A Waste." He scored twice as high on the SAT at the age of nine than I did at eighteen. My eyes always go to the ceiling whenever I try to describe his smile, because it was cunning and it was candlelight and practically commanded its own sound effect: *Foomf!* or *Schwoom!* or something.

The relationship at that point began and ended with an intellectually charged high-five in class one day when we met to discuss a Marion-bashing feminist theology essay. Marco threw it down on his desk, roaring, "Cast it into the flames!" and was only maybe forty-five percent kidding, and I called everyone's attention to the page containing the sentence that read along the lines of, "'In my Catholic grade school, Mary was a stick used to beat the smart girls with,'" and I waved the book around and said, "Honey, if you're so *smart*, why are you ending a sentence *with a preposition?*"

I think Marco and I ran into one another at Mass in the Basilica, or at the Grotto, or some other horribly ironic place; I forget exactly how it happened. The point is we met up and we had coffee and coffee turned into nightcaps and talking and eyes welling up and a back rub and, of course, Doing Things.

I cried the entire time.

We didn't do *The* Thing, which even Randal and I didn't do, but it was certainly a far cry from coffee, and the next night we met at Saint Mary's, in the soft humidity of night, him pacing as he smoked a cigarette, me sitting on the steps of the Moreau Center of the Performing Arts with my chin in my hands, watching.

"I wanted to ask you to a dance, you know," I said.

"Why didn't you?"

"Well—when you first started talking to me a couple weeks into class, and I asked which dorm you lived in, you told me Old College."

"So?"

"*So?* That's the *seminary!*"

"The preliminary program," he said, waving the cigarette at me, "for undergraduates *considering* the seminary." Another puff. "They encourage us to date, actually. Just to make sure."

"Just to make sure," I echoed, so fiercely attracted I was surprised the air around me wasn't shimmering with a glowing plasma, wild electrons with nowhere to go.

Smoking was my number-one turnoff.

"I would have said yes," he said. "I'm sorry you missed the dance on my account."

"Oh—I still went."

There was a pause. "Who'd you ask?"

I leaned against the banister, eyes fixed on the trees. "Randal."

He crushed out the cigarette. "God. Don't tell him, okay. I know him from the Basilica. He's a good guy. He doesn't have to find out. This goes no further, you and me."

"It can't."

"That's what I'm telling you."

He kissed me.

We went to Confession the next morning.

Marco sought out his superior. I found a priest at the Basilica, stared into the heavy vestments pooling at his feet, and started talking.

✳ ✳ ✳

I paced the Grotto, the parking lots, the Avenue, for the rest of the summer. I screamed inhospitably at campers. I needed to tell him, to discover if I could do something *this bad* to another human being and not shatter on impact.

"Don't tell him," said one of my co-workers. She was healing a tattoo on her abdomen at the moment, and was peering down her shorts to check the bandages.

"Don't tell him," said my supervisor when I was forced to explain my gritty eyes, the baseball cap shoved low, the feet that were never still the next day at work.

I told him. Four months later, in October, behind the dumpster at his dorm.

The conversation went like this:

"What's wrong with you? You haven't been yourself since school started. Tell me."

"Don't dump me—"

"Huh?"

"Ichuowahregta..."

"*What?* Why would I— You're shaking. Why are you shaking? What's wrong?"

"I...cpoaisdghaw...."

"You're *pregnant?*"

"No! I *cheated*... last summer...on you...Oh God... I'm sorry... I'm so sorry..."

Silence can be very loud sometimes.

"Did you—"

"*No.*"

"Well." He finally dropped his arms at his sides, relief pouring from the fingertips. "At least you're not pregnant."

He did not dump me.

✳ ✳ ✳

Randal hated my perms. *"Straight* hair," he used to say when I went at the flatter parts of it with a curling iron. "Why can't you just let your hair be as it is?"

I had the perm chemically removed at the end of the summer, a week before he was due to return to school and two days prior to my parents' arrival to help me move into my dorm room for the new school year. For the first time since I was twelve, it hung in limp, fine locks, straight from the crown past my shoulder blades.

On the day my parents arrived, I greeted them in my best working dress and spun. "My new hair," I said. "What do you think?"

My mother's eyes, they were watering. "It—you…"

"I straightened it!"

"Beth—it's *green.*"

My supervisor recommended a salon in Michigan. The summer of chlorine and the agents in the straightening chemicals, said the hairdresser, had killed the bottom two thirds of my hair. It happened so slowly that I hadn't even noticed.

"It's *dead,*" she announced, suspending a blonde mushy clump between her fingertips.

I glanced at my mother in the mirror, then looked away. Someone on the outside had finally seen it, the decay I didn't even know I'd been carrying with me, the damage I'd done.

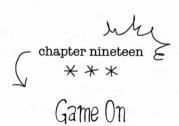

chapter nineteen

✳ ✳ ✳

Game On

I am a perfunctory hockey fan; one who roots when the situation demands but who otherwise cannot be bothered. The goal buzzer is entirely too loud, and anything outside of a spacewalk that requires four hours to get dressed cannot possibly be worth all that trouble.

I was also a properly perfunctory fan in college, where in Section Seven of Notre Dame's hockey arena, my male friends and I managed to raise heckling to an art form. Screaming was the only acceptable form of communication. There was no multicultural awareness. There were no "I...you" statements. There was only yelling.

When thus packed together, we were known as the Goon Squad. The Goons were not merely a pack of obnoxious, college drunks. No. There was no drinking before entering into the sanctum of Section Seven, for alcohol dulled the senses. One was forced to be quick on the uptake in order to maximize instantaneous heckling abilities.

Oh, we were proactive community members indeed. I'd like to point to the following public services the Goon Squad provided at a Notre Dame-Western Michigan game in my senior year:

A good-faith attempt to stabilize international relations
Immediately following "The Star-Spangled Banner," the Squad

struck up a moving a cappella rendition of "O Canada," one Goon
holding lyrics aloft before us on a large wipe-off board. We indeed
struck a blow for world peace that evening: as we sang, the Glee
Club, which had performed the American national anthem, stood
rooted to the ice, stunned; the arena announcer held off on a vital
bulletin concerning the availability of Papa John's coupons in our
programs; the players, lined up at attention at center ice, let us get
all the way to the "With glowing hearts we see thee rise" point
before realizing that this was not in fact an official pre-game event
and they were losing valuable skate-around-while-banging-your-
sticks time; and the entire population of the bleachers remained
standing, providing generous applause when we were finished,
probably because they couldn't see the enormous "EH?" someone
added to the end of the lyrics on the wipe-off board.

Creating a welcoming atmosphere for our opponents

We achieved this via a series of cordial salutations flung in
the general direction of the visitor's bench, or, in especially tender
moments, the penalty box. At times we added a warm personal
touch by welcoming our guests by name:

"YOU SUCK!"

"HEY! HEY RAGUSETT! WE SAW YOU BLOW THE GAME
     LAST NIGHT! AND YOU'RE GOING TO DO IT AGAIN
     TONIGHT! YOU HAVE NO INTRINSIC WORTH, YOU
     GODLESS PUNK!"

"HOEY! WHAT ARE YOU GONNA DO FOR A FACE WHEN
     THE BABOON WANTS HIS ASS BACK? HUH? WHAT
     WILL YOU DO?"

"I KNOW YOU CAN HEAR ME, RAGU!"

"MICHIGAN'S NOT EVEN A REAL STATE ANYWAY, AM
     I RIGHT?"

"SCHMIDT! EVERYONE HATES YOU! YOUR TEAM
     HATES YOU! YOUR MOTHER HATES YOU! EVEN
     THE ACLU HATES YOU! BUT WE DON'T HATE
     YOU... BECAUSE YOU SUCK!"

"HEY HOEY! WE DIDN'T FORGET ABOUT YOU, HOEY!
     YOU SUCK, YOU UGLY PIECE OF GARBAGE!"
"DANCE FOR ME, SCHMIDT! WANG-CHUNG TONIGHT!
     COME ON! I WANNA SEE YOU GET JIGGY WITH IT!"
"I KNOW YOU CAN HEAR ME!"

Equal-opportunity heckling

Heckling is by and large a male-dominated field, but I was received with open lungs in Section Seven. The presence of a female voice opened an entirely new realm of insult possibilities. I would scream things like "HEY MICHIGAN! I AM NOT IMPRESSED BY THE SIZE OF YOUR STICKS!"

Raising awareness of over-the-counter cures for certain medical conditions

"Prune juice!" we sang after the opening bars of "Wild Thing" blasted tinnily through the arena. "You make my bowels loose! You make everything soupy!"

The Glee Club, which joined us at the end of the second period, applauded.

Making the opposing team's goalie and the referee aware of the blatant promiscuity of his sister and/or mother

This was a most popular and well-received Goon Squad service, and we broached this delicate topic in only the most sensitive of terms:

"REF! GO BACK TO SCREWING YOUR MOTHER SO
     YOU'LL STOP SCREWING US!"
"HEY, HOEY! WHAT'S THE DIFFERENCE BETWEEN
     YOUR SISTER AND A SOUTH BEND CITY BUS?
     IT COSTS MORE TO RIDE THE BUS!"
"SCHMIDT! I SAW YOUR MOTHER ON A STREET
     CORNER LAST NIGHT! I WAS GOING TO GET
     WITH HER, BUT THE GUY IN FRONT OF ME
     HAD CORRECT CHANGE!"
"HEY, HOEY! WHAT'S THE OTHER DIFFERENCE

BETWEEN YOUR SISTER AND A SOUTH BEND CITY BUS? TEN POUNDS!"

"SPEAKING OF YOUR SISTER, HOEY, YOU EVER SEE NAKED PICTURES OF HER? YOU WANNA SEE MINE?"

As always, we were just trying to help.

Providing a wave of support for all Notre Dame athletes

The Squad received a bonus that night, for a fencing meet was finishing up behind the stands in the hour before the hockey game began. This provided excellent pre-game entertainment and unparalleled warm-up heckling opportunities:

"THAT'S NOT A *SPORT!*"

"WE'RE MORE ENTERTAINED WATCHING THE ICE DRY!"

"MY NAME IS INIGO MONTOY... aw, screw it, it's too easy."

"I BET WHEN YOU WOKE UP THIS MORNING YOU THOUGHT YOU WOULDN'T HAVE PEOPLE YELLING AT YOU WHILE YOU WERE TRYING TO FENCE! WELL— YOU WERE WRONG!"

And in the middle of the game, we made a positive identification of then-head football coach Bob Davie, who was sitting directly across the ice from us. He'll deny it on record, but he totally waved at us after repeated screamings of "COACH! IT'S ME, RUDY! LET ME DRESS FOR THE GAME! SOON I'LL BE AN OFFICIAL NOTRE DAME STUDENT!"

We weren't serious, though. No football for us. We needed to conserve our wind for the next face-off.

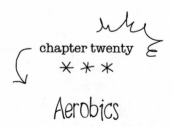

chapter twenty

* * *

Aerobics

There was a legend, entirely urban, circulating the campus that the administration, in an effort to combat eating disorders, chemically soaked the dining hall food with double the calories of normal food. So you could make a peanut butter and jelly sandwich at the sandwich bar, which in other circumstances might be worth maybe 350 or 400 calories, but *this* food, the Saint Mary's food, would land you on daytime television, one of those women who got into awful car wrecks but the paramedics were unable to airlift out of the twisted metal because the helicopter couldn't get off the ground with you in the cargo hold.

I never bought into this; first of all, women with eating disorders never ate peanut butter and jelly to begin with, or else tossed it right back up at the sandwich bar. A couple of my friends did gain a pound or two from what I could notice, but the fact that they lived on entire pitchers of beer and Papa John's consumed at three AM might have been contributing factors more than the Dread Peanut Butter of Lardosity.

One of Saint Mary's primary selling points is that her students, without any men to set our makeup guns to WhoreTastic for, are free to concentrate on academics rather than our appearance. This was true, Monday through Friday; I once attended a 9 AM class in shower shoes and a fuzzy knee-length tee shirt featuring Snoopy wearing a Reds baseball cap, and was overdressed for the occasion.

But there was a gym on campus and the cardio equipment was hard to come by in the late afternoons, with French majors and sophomore class presidents and the co-founder of SMC Pride Week bobbing up and down, up and down on the Stairmasters and elliptical trainers, millions of miles to nowhere, anatomy notes propped up before them and mix tapes on the Sony Walkmen. We had enormous foam earphones and a gym dress code; jog bras, yes, but only under a tee shirt, where they belonged. Stay fit, ladies, and watch your weight, but don't *look* like you're watching your weight. Self-obsess casually in this place where *The New Yorker* is shoved next to *Cosmo* in the campus mailboxes.

I was a senior just as ripped abs became the thing, when women were suddenly supposed to have developed the ability to win a seat in the Senate and tow the Washington Monument around using only our midsections. There was a great deal of talk about "using your core" and "lifting from the *in*side;" all I knew was my lower abdomen was starting to do this weird poochy thing it hadn't in high school, and I was terrified, and ashamed of my terror, here at my women's college where I was supposed to be worried about Tibet and fuel injection buildup rather than the poochy state of my abdomen, so when I signed up for a phys ed class called 'Glutes 'n' Guts', I also wrote a big long essay about how Madonna was a very terrible role model (the pop slut, not the original, Jesus-having one) in order to make myself feel better about the whole affair.

If you want to get a bunch of Catholics to do something, the best course of action is to put them in an enormous line. This is what the Glutes 'n' Guts instructor did—she had us lay down on our backs on the upper level of the campus gym, eyes to ceiling and God and wax-papery skylights. We trapped our feet beneath a heavy orange guardrail, and *crunched*. Crunch. Crunch. Then we did walking squats around the whole entire basketball court, and then we went to breakfast and had maple syrup on the side.

Normally I kept in shape entirely by accident and by jogging, wild, music-driven careens down the Avenue that took me around

the lakes at Notre Dame and back. Sometimes I put on a pair of
in-line skates, flailing past the front of Le Mans and unlacing
the boots when I got to the intersection of Route 33, scampering
over to Notre Dame territory in tube socked feet and returning
to a wheeled state once I was free of the dangerous intersection.
These were mental health excursions, stress blowouts more
than an attempt to define waistlines or reshape thighs or run in
terror from the supposedly fat-globbed dining hall bagels. But
this business with the Glutes 'n' Guts—this was sculpting, was
changing my body.

In a few weeks, after pulling my spring clothes from the back
of my closet, I began to notice that some of my dresses weren't
fitting right, the size eights from the Junior Department, designed
for people without hips or boobs, stretching oddly across my upper
abdominals. I was bursting out of my clothes, the striations of new
muscle hard against the little pink and yellow floral prints, and this
also horrified me. One hour, three times a week. Good for the body,
good for the brain circulation and the Washington Monument-
hoisting. These were liberated abs, and to maintain them would
require me to forevermore donate a minimum of one hour, three
times a week on the upper level of the campus gym.

I sat in my Gender in World Politics class, arching into sensible
pastel tops recently purchased from the clearance rack of the Career
Miss Department. I was twenty-two, now, and in a job search, and
my new abs had given me an excuse to graduate up the escalator to
the women's floor of the department store. What had worked at a
dorm party would not work at the Career Fair.

At the end of the course I borrowed a full-length mirror from
Carah and stripped down and stood in front of it. Hips and curves
and cellulite beginning at the thighs, upper abs in graded ridges,
bottom region still pooching. Was I more of a woman now, or less?
I alternately sucked in and slouched out, amused and amazed at
the difference a straight-shouldered posture could create. I weighed
more than I did in high school but less than I would in four years,
when a corporate door would clank shut behind me and I mainlined

Nestle's Quick in order to stay awake and consolable.

Well, the canned music in the Junior Department was poundingly obnoxious anyway, I'd begun to notice. I flipped the mirror over and put on an old tee shirt and a pair of sneakers and got on the elliptical trainer, *The New Yorker* propped up in front of me.

chapter twenty-one

* * *

Stripping the Wire

My brother school had a radio station, WVFI-AM. It had a broadcast radius of two and a half dorms, and until we had to go off the air because our CD player broke, I read the news at noon.

I also served as WVFI's Saint Mary's Liaison Officer. This largely consisted of posting flyers for the station's 80's Lunch Hour, which was broadcast once a semester live from Saint Mary's dining hall, and I tell you now that nothing says "higher education" like chicken fingers congealing to the beat of "Come On Eileen."

One year some fool put me in charge of printing the flyers, so I found various shades of fluorescent paper and reprinted the lyrics of 80's songs, including Cyndi Lauper's "She-Bop," which I thought was an adorable idea until somebody pulled me aside and explained, very gently, that in this particular work Cyndi was not exactly singing about riding a motorcycle.

I fared slightly better in the broadcast booth. What I would do was, at 11:59 AM, go to the station's news office—this consisted entirely of a fax machine sitting on a set of cardboard drawers in the corner of a booth—and "strip the wire", or "uncurl the news copy from the wire service or fish it out of the trash where the 11 AM broadcaster had tossed it, whichever place I thought to look first."

In the middle of the broadcast, I did a weather report, which in South Bend typically consisted of the words "dropping" and "wind chill." Whichever DJ happened to man the board at the moment was in charge of cuing up the "weather bed," which was a series of dramatic keyboard zaps and drum-intensive music, because when it came to revealing the local dewpoint, The People *could not wait.*

(Zapzapzapzapzap*zap)* "Local South Bend temperature twenty-two degrees," I would say, (drumdrumdrumdrum*drum)* "with a wind chill factor of twelve" (keyboard roar). "Flurries expected in the afternoon hours" (druuuuuuuum) "and an overnight low of eight." (ZAP!)

Less exciting was the actual news. We had no zapping for that. It was supposed to zap for itself.

On my first day as a newscaster, I stripped the wire, shook off the potato chip crumbs from The News, and bent over the blurry words, cramming a bagel down my throat and ordering the stories. The first story, the suggested lead headline, was something important and galaxy-bending, I'm sure, and I could not tell you what it was for all the chardonnay in Napa. The second lead was slightly less vital for day-to-day existence, and I can't remember that one, either.

The third, though—the third lead seemed more appropriate for a college audience. I wiped poppy seeds off my red pen and circled it, arrowing it to the top of the page. Between Saint Mary's exchange program with American University and Notre Dame's reputation as a law school funnel, one of our main exports was Washington-bound interns.

So the first words out of my mouth as an Official Member of the Broadcast Media were: "An Internet gossip site called 'The Drudge Report' alleges today that President Clinton may have had an inappropriate relationship with a college intern."

The DJ whose show began after my broadcast had to duck under the board so that my microphone wouldn't pick up his laughter. "You read that Clinton rumor one again," he whispered over the weather bed, "read it again, because it'll be the last we'll ever hear of it. There's no way that story is true. *No one* is *that* horny."

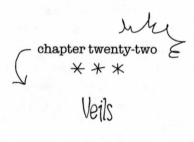

chapter twenty-two
* * *

Veils

I n my senior year, I went away for spring break.

Most college students pass senior spring break in an alcoholic stupor, strewing underwear across the Florida panhandle and entire bathtubs of wine coolers. It's never a good spring break unless you find yourself back on campus with unexplained bruises on one hand and a release form for *Girls Gone Wild* in the other.

Me, I went to Latin Mass.

Patty, Grace, and I booked ourselves in a hotel that the chain's homepage described as located "in the heart of Orlando's shopping district," and we, stupidly, did not instantly question what one might be shopping *for*. We had been encountering billboards advertising an enterprise entitled "Fiona's Fantasy Wear" for miles, which we found hilarious, until we discovered that Fiona's Fantasy Wear was located approximately eight feet away from the hotel pool.

Other conveniently located establishments included:

"XXX Adult Factory Outlet"

"The Boobie Bungalow"

"Miss Elise's Club for Fine Gentlemen."

Two blocks down from the Heart of Orlando's Shopping District, we happened upon exactly what you might expect: a Catholic church. I had been appointed the Religious Coordinator of the group— largely because I was the one who made the widely hailed discovery that Catholics traveling on Fridays in Lent are excused from meat abstention and fasting—so, "Mandy's Thong Outlet" at my back, I peered through the frosted doors of St. Monica's of the Water, which had no kneelers or visible tabernacle but a very healthy schedule of Masses in Esperanto.

This left us with Sacred Heart Traditional Parish, which was seven blocks and forty years in the other direction. This place had kneelers, all right. It also had High Mass candles, a pack of nuns in full habit, and a big scary sign in the back reading "LET ALL MORTAL FLESH BE SILENT."

Also, chapel veils.

I've often wondered how my generation, the first born into a post-Vatican II world, would fare if we were ever dropped into the Church culture that raised our parents. We were brought up in an America in which the University of Notre Dame bookstore sells watercolors that feature small children playing soccer with Jesus. (Oh, there's a whole line of them. He plays a variety of sports with these kids; apparently, the Messiah is quite the cross-trainer.)

I now know *exactly* what we would do: We would put our chapel veils on sideways.

Chapel veils, as I understand them, are lace headpieces that women were expected to wear inside a church if they had no other head covering. There was a basket of them at the church entrance, and we were looking at nothing but the lace-covered backs of female heads, so we put our near-degrees to work and plopped them on. Patty tried to tie hers under her chin, Grace Kelly kerchief-style; I got mine tangled up in a necklace and spent the entire Mass dangling a tiny space shuttle charm from the side of my head.

You truly do not know your friends until you have seen them in chapel veils. We looked like five year olds playing wedding, and all of us insisted upon being the bride.

"We are all going to hell," Grace said to me out of the side of her mouth as we perched, terrified, on a marble kneeler. The hems of our skirts, while well out of Fiona's Fantasy Wear range, stopped significantly short of our knees.

Patty took in the Papal and American flags on the altar and, like all post-Vatican II Catholics, immediately associated large banners with long Mass length and started to panic. "Are you sure this is only going to take an hour?" she hissed.

I picked up a missal, curious as to what was sung here.

Wha—? Where were the hymns?

I flipped farther. There were just... words. Foreign words.

Oh God!

It was going to be in Latin!

The whole thing!

"How are we supposed to know when to hold hands during the Our Father?" Grace asked me as soon as word spread.

I shook my head, one hand clamped over my chapel veil. "I don't think we have to worry about that."

The Mass was a large-scale, Catholic version of Simon Says. We were always at least two genuflections and one *Deus* behind everybody else. As we watched the rest of the congregation head for the Communion rail at the front of the church, I sent "Don't put your hands out! Don't put you hands out! We have to take the Host on the tongue!" down the line.

"What? Why?"

"We have to go up to the altar and kneel at the Communion rail!" I hissed.

"The *what?*"

"Just do whatever the nuns are doing!"

We processed to the front of the church, attempting as we did so to simultaneously lower hemlines and raise necklines. The priest approached us, muttering Latin, vestments heavy.

"You," whispered Patty kneeling next to me, shoving her chapel veil out of her face, "are frickin' *fired* as the Religious Coordinator."

chapter twenty-three

* * *

Welcome Center

Carah and I sat at lunch. She was wearing an engagement ring. I was wearing jeans from Wal-Mart. Our necklaces, though, with the Saint Mary's seal on the topside—those were the same.

We were both home in Cincinnati for Christmas.

"Are you going to the five-year reunion?" she said.

I shook my head. "I'm teaching summer classes."

"Really?" She put down her glass of orange juice. "When's the last time you were back on campus?"

I thought. "October? October of—okay, it was the first home football game after 9/11, so it had to be..." I shrugged. "Too long. The Avenue looked weird anyway. Have you seen the new building they put up?"

"I think—is that the Welcome Center, that little cottage-looking thing by the side of the road? With the—"

"With the French cross inlaid on the blonde wood floor, yeah," I finished. "Now I know why I got a bill every time I needed a transcript for a grad school application."

"How are things going with that gu—"

"Dumped him."

"Oh."

"I told him I wanted to have my first book tour before my thirtieth birthday, and he laughed, so I said, 'I'm slowing down the car, and you have five seconds to jump out before I *push* you out, at which point I won't be going so slowly.'"

"I'm sorry."

"So's he."

"I wish you could come to campus with me. I'll get a picture of your old dorm room in Regina."

I shook my head. "Don't. I never went back to Two North, after freshman year."

"Are you serious?"

"I would not lie about a Two North-related paradigm shift. I have not set foot in that hallway since the day I walked out of it at the end of freshman year with a sophomore class schedule and an empty box of pantyliners."

"Seriously?"

"I don't want to see it belonging to anybody else. I don't want to stir the cosmic landscape. Kind of like how there's no atmosphere on the Moon, so Neil Armstrong's first footprint is still exactly as he left it? Like that."

"It's just unlike you to not grab on to every little thing you can of the place."

"Yeah, well…my arms are getting full."

"Don't you miss it?"

"Oh, I do, I do." I flicked away the little paper ball I'd made of a straw wrapper. "It's just that I don't think I could crawl my way up those walls anymore. Remember how I told you the doctor said I might need knee surgery? From standing in high heels when I lecture during class?"

Carah tipped her head to the table. *"What,"* she said, "happened to that girl I met at Orientation who didn't want to go see a movie with me? What was it you said? 'I don't trust that Tom Hanks'?"

"I have *not changed.*"

"Oh," she said, "I think you have."

"Shut up."

She looked up at me. "Let's just say you're a little more willing to open a door these days."

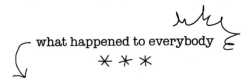
what happened to everybody

* * *

Saint Mary's College: Somehow did not crumble into Lake Michigan after I graduated.

The University of Notre Dame: I understand that's still there, too.

Belles: There was an attempt in my senior year to abolish the name in exchange for "The Banshees" or something equally self-hating. "Belles" held firm. The year after I graduated, somebody in Student Government fashioned a gigantic over-the-head paper mache bell with a small slit for eyes to be worn at home basketball games. Then they painted it blue. I understand people fight over who gets to wear it. I also understand that I will not be donating to the Student Government Fund Drive for a while.

Anne: Two years ago, I called her, saying, "I think I need to apologize for the entirety of sophomore year." We email all the time these days. She even proofread this manuscript, which may explain how very nicely she comes off in "Roommates."

SYR: They're gone now, replaced by something called an "in-hall dance," which, as I understand it, are predicated on drafting blind dates via friends and roommates. This often results in an alcohol-soaked arranged marriage with a duration of perhaps four hours, which culminates in drunken, grabby not-sex and never speaking to the lady or gentleman in question again.

Carah: She became a reference librarian at the National Archives, then married her white knight, who whisked her away to his castle in Scotland. I was a bridesmaid.

Okay, it's a regular three-bedroom house. But still. For Carah, it's a *castle*. In *Scotland*.

Kathy: She, too, is married, with 2.95 babies, so she's pretty much still getting twenty minutes of sleep every four years.

Amy: I ran into her at a football game in 2001. I think she's in law school now, which is why I changed her name before this went to press.

Patty: Married her high school sweetheart and has two little boys. I do not think the Mickey Mouse poster is anywhere near the nursery.

Edmonds: TEACHES GRADE SCHOOL IN SHECAAAAAHH-HHHHH-GO.

Justine: She's married with a little girl, and back in Cleveland, where she and her hot plate can live without fear.

Dead Fetal Pig: Man. I really don't even want to think about what kind of condition the dead fetal pig is in by now.

University of Notre Dame Glee Club: Still singing and boozing, because, as it turns out, harmonizing and drinking actually do mix. As a member of the Saint Mary's College Women's Choir, I sang *Carmina Burana* with them and the South Bend Symphony Orchestra when I was a senior. I'm so relived we could work together on a professional basis after all the sexual tension.

The Club just released a new CD they recorded on campus. A little Broadway, a little Victory March; it's a beautiful album, strong on the tenors. They sound very young.

Grace: She married soon after we graduated—Patty was in her wedding—and served as an Army nurse at Walter Reed. She has three babies. I imagine they don't cross her.

Regina Hall: Regina has since been expanded to double rooms and "shingles," which sounds like a horrible social disease but actually refers to "shared singles," in which two girls share three cells between them. I would like to see that. But not experience it.

The Notre Dame Leprechaun: Jamey graduated in my freshman year and vanished into a Golden Dome sort of Camelot mist, for I never heard from him again. He's doing push-ups somewhere in Brigadoon, I imagine.

Frances Davidson Trenton: Is very likely either currently incarcerated or the next member of the United States Supreme Court. Possibly both.

Indiana, The State Of: Still flat.

Randal: Is not a priest. He married a cheerleading coach and is a high school vice principal, or so I've been told fourth-hand. As with all my exes, I say unto him: Sorry about the panic attacks and thanks for all the non-sex.

Marco: Isn't a priest either. I Googled him (Google was invented, I strongly believe, solely to address our deep-seated need to confirm that we are currently living infinitely better lives than those of former romantic partners) and it turns out he's doing some Very Important management-consulting sort of thing, and is pretty much walking wallet-lopsided from all the bank he's currently pulling. I hear—this is the *best*—I hear that he's advising the Congregation of the Holy Cross *pro bono* on meeting vocation recruitment goals.

You know how some women have a propensity to date closeted gay men? I do that with almost-priests. Sorry, Catholic Church. You suck 'em in, I pull 'em *right* back out.

U.S. Route 33: It was under construction for the whole of my college career, inching its way up Indiana year after year, with the last orange barrel retrieved from the Saint Mary's–Notre Dame intersection the weekend I graduated. My mother read in the paper last week that it needs repairs again.

The Observer: When I was a senior, the offices were moved to the basement of Notre Dame's South Dining Hall. This severely hampered our Official News Collecting Abilities. The only thing worse than writing by college students is writing by college students against the backdrop of lingering Eau de Leftover Corndogs.

My abs: That Glutes 'n' Guts six-pack vanished within a two-month period in 2002, when I was working eighteen hour days and dinner consisted of an entire pizza at one in the morning. You can't *do* that and continue to rock out with your bad-self abs. Come back, abs.

Regis Philbin: Regis went on to become my classmate. He was presented with an honorary doctorate in 1999 and is not returning my calls.

Two North: It became like Margaritaville after we were freshmen, more a state of mind than an actual place. Last year was the tenth anniversary of the year we met. We tried to have a reunion at Saint Mary's, but everybody was too busy being pregnant and grown-up. And you know what, if all of us we really *were* able to instantaneously drop our lives and hurl ourselves northward for a weekend, then Saint Mary's had likely done a crap job with us, for this would have meant we were all residing in hollowed-out Volkswagen vans, living off the ecosystem.

Mary Beth Ellis: I earned a Master of Fine Arts in creative writing, which did not require any math, and then did exactly what would you would expect a person to do with a Master of Fine Arts in creative writing: I landed a day job in education at the Kennedy Space Center, because, as it happens, NASA *does* have a need for professional evaluators of Jane Austen. Now I write for an enormously useless website, BlondeChampagne.com, and teach writing at an aeronautical university, at which I sit whenever and wherever I want.

The student body population is 85% male.

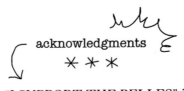

acknowledgments
✳ ✳ ✳

A complimentary "I SUPPORT THE BELLES" jogbra goes to:

Josh Hunter, my most ardent fan and pilot-turned-proofreader, who endured such non-aviation inquires as "Is this funnier with or without the ellipses?"

Andy Dehnart of realityblurred.com and the Bennington Bitch Society, who introduced me to such lifechanging entities as 0% interest balance transfers, the very first department head to offer me a teaching position, Mp3 players, my editor at MSNBC.com, and this zany new thing all the kids are doing called "blogging." Basically, without Andy, I'd be infinitely more pathetic than I actually am, and the world just does not need that.

Mike "The Longterm Reader" Marchand, who provided a Domer perspective on an early draft and had the testicular fortitude to inform me that it… really kind of sucked.

Ryan "The Rocket Scientist" Geoffroy, who worked his computer-y mojo and unlocked many memories by managing to access thousands of words of old, bad, Mac-based writing I hadn't seen in about a decade. At the time, for some reason, I thought this would be a good thing.

Carah Smith Tabar, The BFFE, who, from her castle in Scotland, offered to retype every single awful word of a 195-page hard copy original draft if Ryan proved unable to conjure an "open" command on the dusty Mac crap.

Cappy Gagnon, who wrote some of my very first fan mail and saw to it that I was able to smack the golden "Play Like a Champion Today" sign in Notre Dame's locker room, sit two rows behind Gelman and Mrs. Regis Philbin at '99 graduation, and slip backstage at the WWF campus show. I am deeply grateful for the first two and still trying to forgive him for the last.

Elisabeth Krick, who kindly provided a last-minute copyedit session and pointed out such minor continuity flaws as "Why does Carah walk out of your room and back in again, and then two pages later nobody's seen her all day?"

Mrs. Carol T. Dressman, English teacher, lately of Mother of Mercy High School, who suggested Notre Dame to me, and when I laughed very hard and said my writing demanded something smaller, a liberal arts school, perhaps a women's college, she said, "Have you heard of the sister school across the street?"

✳ ✳ ✳

I offer my deepest thanks for the continued moral support of these and other Saint Mary's professors who for some reason refused to run very far away even after I left their care:

Dr. Kevin "Judgemental As Hell" McDonnell

Dr. Joe "I'm Eager To Teach You, Only Not During *Seinfeld*" Incandella

Dr. Laura "Oscar Wilde? Gay" Haigwood

Kerry Temple, editor of *Notre Dame Magazine*, who remembered me several years after graduation and emailed one day to ask if I had written anything lately. I was trapped in an engineering firm's cubicle in Orlando and was miserable and hadn't. He told me that if I was willing to get off my butt for a thousand words, he would give me a check. I did, and he did, and from that day forward, I began to circulate white blood cells again.

The delightful and ever ego-stroking **Dr. Max Westler,** who deeply impacted my work ethic where my own future professorial career was concerned when we walked into his classroom one day and found that he had written the following on the blackboard: "It started to snow and I got scared, so I went home."

I am ever grateful to and humbled by my faithful **The Readers at BlondeChampagne.com,** who clicked on the Amazon Honor System banner and battled trolls and left extraordinarily kind comments that often contained better writing than what was on the actual webpage. Don't get cocky, The Readers.

✳ ✳ ✳

Eternal Aunt-Love goes to **Jim The Small Child Nephew,** my godson, and the baby who held up this whole entire manuscript so I could get his name in here, **William Ronald The Newborn Nephew,** although I kind of doubt he or his brother will attend Saint Mary's. My beautiful sister, **Julie,** my CPA heroine who got to our mother's womb first and sucked out all the mathematical competency genes, has always deferred to me in word-heavy work, saying, *"You're* the creative one." Well, I've written a real live book, now, and when I typed the last chapter I sat here feeling quite smug about myself until I realized that a lifetime's worth of bestsellers will never come close to rivaling the creative masterpieces that are her sons. Get a load of my big sister, you guys. *She* makes *people.*

Printed in the United States
147813LV00003B/1/A

9 781583 851067